Edible Wild Plants

Cookbook and Foraging Guide

*A Guidebook to Foraging, Harvesting, Identifying and Cooking
Essential Wild Food, With 100 Recipes for Making The Best Use Of
Edible Wild Plants For Your Overall Health.*

Abbey Miller

Contents

Warning

Preservation Methods

Transporting Wild Edible Plants

Selecting the Site

Growing Guidelines

Farming Your Plants

Soil

Water

Introduction

Do you want to learn more about foraging and how to gather and cook wild plants? Are you interested in learning how to recognize these plants, their health advantages, and how to grow them yourself? Foraging in the wild and harvesting edible wild plants are the subject of this book.

People's desire to reconnect with nature and disconnect from contemporary technology is a relatively new phenomenon. More sustainable food sources are being sought since people are aware of the delicate nature of the world. An incresing number of people are opting for a plant-based diet, and as their numbers grow, so does the demand for organic plant sources to help them spice up their everyday meals. Unless you've lived under a rock for several years, you've grown tired of the same old grocery store fare. Look for items that are healthful, sustainable, and cost-effective when you're making food. Organic food is becoming increasingly common, but it can be pricey and hard to come by.

Foraging has grown in popularity in recent years due to these factors. Get some fresh air and work out in the great outdoors while boosting your natural capacity to grow food. If you want to learn to recognize a wide range of wild-harvested ingredients that you may utilize in your cooking, this is the book for you. Understanding foraging and learning the tools needed to choose wild plants will be taught in this book. If you want to grow wild plants in your backyard, you'll need to read this book for some helpful advice. In this book, you'll learn how to plant your seeds, what tools you need, and how to maintain your garden.

Every day, you won't be foraging for food. Wild plants can be found in your yard, on a sidewalk, in parks, or the nearby forests and wild areas, depending on where you are. But not everyone has this luxury, so they must travel to a location where foraging is legal. Keeping wild plants as fresh as possible is a must because of this. You can learn how to preserve and store wild plants for a long period by reading this book. Additionally, you'll need to learn how to properly store the plants, so they don't go bad.

Certain wild plants have the same fruits, veggies, and seeds that you can buy in the supermarket. Because you're already familiar with them, you can easily include them in your cooking. However, you may not know how to use other wild herbs in your cooking. So, we put a few recipes in the book to demonstrate how you can use various unique things found in nature to brighten and spice up your meals.

Several of these wild plants have incredible therapeutic properties. Foraging is a fantastic way to ensure you get the greatest possible plants. Fresher, pesticide- and fertilizer-free vegetables are impossible to find. Natural selection has developed wild plants, which is why they are so valuable. Even if organic, natural fruits and veggies taste better than anything, you'll find in a supermarket, even if grown in a greenhouse. After reading this book, you will want to go out and forage for wild plants and incorporate them into your daily meals.

This book is an exclusive resource for learning how to successfully forage for wild food plants. It's essential to know which plants are safe to eat and which ones are poisonous so that you can avoid consuming them. Let's get started on the world of foraging and how to harvest and cook edible wild plants.

History of Edible Wild Plants

Our society consumes only a small percentage of the world's edible plant species. Recently Botanical estimated that 390,900 plants exist, with at least half of those being edible to humans (United Nations, 2016). There are only roughly 200 plant species that we eat daily. More than half of the calories and proteins we obtain from plants come from only three crops: maize, rice, and wheat. These three crops account for the majority of the plant species we consume.

We don't eat many edible plants because they're low in nourishment. It's also not a matter of taste but because of commercial viability. Farmers choose high-yielding crops that have been genetically modified to withstand pest infestation and assure high yield ratios over traditional crops that have not been altered.

Because of the drastic changes made in labs, the DNA of nearly all genetically modified (GM) plants resembles little to nothing about the original wild plant. While GM seed laboratories promise advantages such as drought resistance, reduced use of pesticides in GM crop production, enhanced agricultural efficiency, resiliency, and profitability, the negative implications of GM crops remain mostly unknown.

Many GM crops have detrimental environmental repercussions, according to scientists. Over 60 million acres of crop farms were lost by herbicide-resistant weeds created by GM crops introduced in 1996. Farmers employed an herbicide called Glyphosate, which kills pollinating insects like bees and butterflies, to fight these superweeds.

Toxicity:

Aside from commercial viability, there are several other reasons why we consume so little of the edible plants. Natural plant species evolution also plays a significant part in this. In order to protect themselves from grazing herbivores, parasitic insects, and fungal infections, most of the world's 390,900 plant species have evolved chemical defences (poisons). More than three-fourths of the world's 390,900 plant species have evolved by developing a chemical defence to protect themselves from herbivores, parasitic insects, and fungal pathogens.

Even the plants we consider the healthiest can be deadly and have many poisonous relatives. The Solanum genus contains nightshade, nettle, and tomatoes and is also home to potatoes, aubergines, and tomatoes (eggplant). All of which are packed with toxic chemicals called alkaloids. Capsaicin, the alkaloid responsible for the hot, burning taste sensation of chilies and peppers developed in the plant to ward off bacteria. Capsaicin is also poisonous to humans because it causes inflammation in our taste buds, stomach, and intestines. And yet, people consume around 118 million pounds of chili annually.

Diversity:

However, there is little evidence to suggest that early civilizations cultivated a broader range of food crops than we see on supermarket shelves today. When it comes to food, early man would have been limited to the wild and domesticated plants that flourished in their area at different times. In addition, there would have been a limited supply of crops and food preservation methods. Refrigeration and aviation have made it possible for us to have access to a wide variety of fresh produce from around the world.

Although we now have plant species unavailable to early civilizations, you're unlikely to find more than twenty of the two hundred species we eat in your local supermarket.

Ethnobotany:

Ethnobotanists and archaeologists believe that Homo erectus began harvesting plant seeds, nuts, fruits, roots, and greens about 1.8 million years ago when predators killed animals and scavenged their carcasses for nourishment.

Stone-age hunting implements have been found dating back 200,000 years, indicating the existence of hunter-gatherers (Homo sapiens). Stone flint knives, arrow tips, axes, fishing nets, hooks, and bone harpoons were some of the more specialized instruments that hunters used. Most hunter-gatherer cultures began to specialize in a larger game, greater quantities of marine species (such as fish and seaweed), and a more limited array of plant-based meals between 70,000 and 80,000 years ago, according to archaeologists.

Most prehistoric hunter-gatherer societies moved about a lot, living in temporary shelters. Animal migrations and the ripening of seasonal plant food sources influenced their movements. They lived in tiny groups of 15 to 30 people and split up further when food became scarce or tribal conflicts erupted. " When the tribes returned to the area, the animals and plants would have recovered and become more numerous due to their migratory habits.

The grassy plains in the Pacific Northwest region of North America were an important source of food for Native American tribes. Especially for the Duwamish, bracken, camas, and Wapato. Ethnobotanists have discovered that the region had one of the only permanently settled hunter-gatherer societies that have ever lived with abundant wild food sources.

Agriculture originated only 12,000 years ago in the Middle East and independently in parts of southern North America and most of Central America. Forest gardening, practiced mostly along riverbanks and on the moist slopes of the mountains, was the first form of agriculture during this time. As tribes gradually improved their farming methods, they discovered and enhanced helpful tree and vine species while eradicating undesirable plant species.

The southern areas of North America were home to the earliest domesticated crops around 5,500 years ago. The Aztec, Maya, and Olmec civilizations harvested crops that included beans, maize (corn), and squash.

Today's commercially grown blackberries barely resemble the wild berries our ancestors ate. Modern cultivar development took place mostly in the United States. In 1880, a hybrid blackberry, named the loganberry, was developed in Santa Cruz, California, by James Harvey Logan. In 1921, the first thornless blackberry varieties were developed but lost much of their flavour. More thornless types developed by the US Department of Agriculture from the 1990s to the beginning of the early 21st century yielded larger fruit with better flavours. These hybrid berries are what is found in the supermarket today.

Medicine & Nutrition:

Individual edible plant species, their seeds, flowers, fruits, and other parts, as well as their traditional medicinal usage, have fascinating histories and lore. For example, the Greeks, other European peoples, and Native Americans employed blackberry plants for traditional medicine—a 1771 document recommended brewing blackberry leaves, stems, and bark for stomach ulcers. The Haraldskaer Woman, a 2,500-year-old bog-preserved body of a Danish woman, is one of the earliest examples of blackberry eating. Blackberries were found in her stomach through forensic evidence. For food, blackberries have been used for a long time in making jams, jellies, and pies. There's a fascinating history behind common weeds like plantain (Plantago major). Some Native American tribes referred to it as a "white man's footprint" because of its ability to thrive in the disturbed and degraded ecosystems surrounding European homesteads once they arrived in North America. Besides plantain's nutritional and medicinal properties, people have been using the weed to heal wounds for over 2,400 years. Plantain leaves were extensively used in traditional medicine to make skin poultices for wounds, ulcers, and insect stings. Fever and respiratory infections were treated with the root. Plantain's antibacterial and wound-healing capabilities have been studied extensively over the last decade. Plantain possesses both antiviral and immune-modulating properties, according to a previous study.

Why You Should Eat Edible Wild Plants?

People have used wild edible plants for thousands of years. Today, many people are interested in eating more natural, local, and organic foods to reduce their carbon footprint and improve their health. Wild edible plants are a natural, healthy choice. Many wild edibles (including some of the most common varieties) have been shown to contain more nutrients than cultivated produce.

The nutritional value of edible wild plants depends on the season, preparation method, and location where they're grown. Each plant will provide varying nutrients and calories based on these factors. For example, several studies have shown that organic foods often contain higher concentrations of essential minerals like iron and zinc than their non-organic counterparts. Eating wild plants also reduces the amount of fertilizer and pesticides used on conventional foods.

Benefits of Eating Edible Wide Plants

There are numerous health benefits of consuming wild plants. Fresh, chemical- and pesticide-free produce from local farmers is a popular choice for many people. Wild edible plants are simply that. They offer fresh, nutritious meals with the smallest environmental footprint possible. Wild edible plants can be a profitable and enjoyable pastime in addition to the obvious health and culinary advantages. It is a way to connect with nature and enjoy exercise outdoors. Some of the benefits of eating wild food can include:

Improved Digestibility:

Many wild edible plants contain little or no cellulose, which makes them easier to digest. The fibre content in wild foods is higher, and it is easier for the body to digest than produce found in the grocery store. So therefore, you will likely experience fewer stomach upset, gas, and constipation after eating wild plant food compared to store-bought fruits and vegetables.

Gastrointestinal Health:

Wild plants have been known to improve the health of the digestive tract. A well-balanced meal from wild plants is a great natural treatment for diarrhoea, constipation, and acid reflux disease. Edible wild plants are known to have anti-inflammatory effects that positively impact the gastrointestinal system. The plants you eat can offer a source of nutrition with low calories. Some contain vegan protein and calcium, which is hard to find in non-edible wild plants.

Cleansing Effect:

The herbal and cleansing effects of all fresh produce help with detoxification from alcohol, drugs, or medication. It can help the body naturally expel these toxins. Wild plants, especially when eaten raw, can help remove harmful toxins from the body. This is an excellent way to remove excess waste and tons of chemicals introduced into the body through everyday foods prepared at restaurants, processed foods, and drinks. The levels of pesticides and herbicides in crops have increased as crops have been genetically engineered to resist them. The body absorbs these chemicals and can cause serious damage if they get into your bloodstream.

Environmental Benefits:

Wild plants are free of pesticides and herbicides. They are often free of fertilizers and other unnatural substances found in non-organic produce. The growing of wild plants has little or no environmental impact. Some wild edible plants are more sustainable to grow than vegetables because they can be grown in a very small space and do not require irrigation, fertilizer, or pesticides.

High in Antioxidants:

Eating wild plants provides vitamins and minerals such as iron, calcium, magnesium, and beta-carotene. All these compounds can fight off free radicals in the body that cause cancer and premature aging.

Rich in Vitamins and Minerals:

Eating wild plants provides essential vitamins and minerals to the body. The structure of wild plants allows them to maintain the vitamins and minerals that are easily perishable. Vitamins in wild plants are more bioavailable than those found in store-bought produce. This makes them easier for the body to absorb, which gives you a superior nutritional value.

Consumption of non-organic foods has been linked to diseases such as cancer, infertility, and Alzheimer's Disease. Wild plants may be the answer to these health problems and countless others.

Edible wild plants have a variety of fruits and greens that are rich in vitamins and minerals, so eating them has many health benefits. Some of the most common wild edible plants are nettle, dandelion, chickweed, raspberry, and mint. Wild edible plants can be part of a healthy diet because they are low in calories and are mostly made of fiber. These plants are rich in vitamins like vitamin C, B complex, and E and minerals like iron, copper, manganese, and magnesium.

According to a study by the University of California at Berkeley, eating wild plants can help reduce the risk of cancer, heart disease, and diabetes. Moringa provides tremendous benefits to the body. It is a powerful anti-inflammatory used to treat many medical conditions, including cancers, arthritis, and diabetes. It also boosts physical fitness.

Calcium Uptake:

The calcium content in edible plants is generally quite high. However, it can be lower than in cow's milk. Very few plants have a high concentration of net calcium (the amount of calcium minus any leaching into the soil). Calcium also has relatively little ascorbate or other antioxidants to bind with it and improve absorption.

Sustainability:

Edible wild plants provide a wealth of free food. Wild food is delicious, whether found in your backyard or far away on a mountain hike. Wild plants are packed with protein, vitamins, minerals, and other nutrients to keep you healthy and energized. After an initial investment in learning identification skills, time spent foraging is free and will surely lead to great meals and a healthier lifestyle.

Stress Relief:

Gathering your wild food can be a very rewarding hobby or a way to de-stress from day-to-day worries. Wild edibles are easily accessible and provide a simple and natural food source. This is a fun way to lose weight to live a healthy, happy life.

Other Health Benefits:

Wild plants can help you lose weight by curbing your appetite. This can be due to plants containing low carbohydrate levels, less than one gram for every 100 grams of the food.

Eating wild food will allow you to experience nature's unique taste and nutrition. You will enjoy feeling that you are connected to your environment while getting a healthier, natural diet at the same time.

What is the Edible Wild plant?

Edible wild plants are not domesticated by humans and grow in the wild. They traditionally have been consumed by the indigenous people who harvested them for food and medicinal purposes in their region. They typically have a milder flavour than their cultivated counterparts and a low toxicity level. They can be used to make incredibly delicious dishes that are good for you too!

Some edible wild plants can be eaten without cooking and have significant nutrients. But not all wild plants found in the woods are edible; many of them are poisonous. That's why it is important to research which plant you will eat before taking that first bite.

Wild plants are important for human survival by providing various nutrients and minerals. They can be eaten raw (green) or processed (cooked). We can use them in soup, juice, tea, corn-starch, or flour.

Many wild plants are used in different conventional and alternative medicines. For example, nettles have anti-inflammatory properties and heal wounds. Soak nettle juice for 20 minutes before dressing the wound to boost its regenerative power. You can also make a face mask out of nettle to eliminate dandruff and pimples.

Some wild plants are used to reduce the pain of arthritis and rheumatism when boiled. Some have analgesic properties, which are useful for toothaches, headaches, and insomnia. Some can be used for purifying the blood and as a diuretic. Dandelion or milk thistle is also used for cleansing the liver.

Edible wild plants are rich in vitamins and minerals such as Vitamin C, A, Iron, Calcium, and Magnesium. They also provide us with essential amino acids. All this is crucial to maintaining our health and immunity.

In the right place in the right quantity, wild plants can be consumed as both food and medicine. The plants have a great impact on our weight loss journey. Our body requires a certain number of calories to keep it functioning properly. Some people are not able to consume enough calories through the foods they eat that they need to stay healthy and fit.

But it won't be a problem if you are strong enough to get a fresh wild plant every day. Your body will get all the nutrition and vitamins required from it.

Find Your Food

Many people are lost when navigating the wilderness and providing food for themselves and their families. Still, anyone can become an expert – all it takes is education.

Wild edible foods were a source of survival for ancient man thousands of years before the development of agriculture. Adding it to one's diet has become a fashionable trend and a healthy method to stay in touch with nature. There are a few things to keep in mind before you get started. Identifying edible wild plants is the subject of this chapter. In addition, the laws of foraging are described, as well as the equipment needed to find wild plants. Foraging food plants, such as fruits, nuts, and flowers, are covered in this guide.

What Is Foraging?

Foraging is the act of gathering, collecting, and consuming wild edible plants. These food sources include plants, herbs, fruits, mushrooms, and flowers that grow around us uncultivated. For thousands of years, people depended on foraged food for survival. However, foraging for food was banned in most parts of the world until the last few centuries.

We benefit from foraging because wild foods provide nutrients and therapeutic characteristics not present in commonly grown foods, which are not available in conventionally grown foods. Modern farmers seek more profitable crops, so many weeds we consider unpleasant are quite nutritious. The availability of wild edible plants in local supermarkets may not be achievable in some situations. Foraging is the best option if you want to eat a wide variety of natural foods or acquire survival skills in the wild.

How to Identify Wild Edible Plants

It is important to determine whether or not a wild plant is edible before consuming it. The universal edibility test is one way to tell if a plant is safe to eat or dangerous because many edible plants look like poisonous ones. You must test the plant on your body to determine if there are any adverse reactions. If the plant is poisonous, this will assist you in avoiding the harmful effects.

The first step in testing wild food is to break it down into smaller, more manageable pieces. Leaves, flowers, seeds, fruits, and roots or bulbs are all edible elements of wild plants. Smell one of the components. If you detect an almond scent, you must avoid that plant. In the same way, acidic and bitter scents are a red flag that something isn't right. Raw plants with a pleasant aroma are generally safe to eat, but you must be careful.

Once you've separated the plant into edible sections, the following step is to conduct a skin test. Use your skin to test whether the plant causes any reaction. Get the juices on your skin by crushing or squeezing leaves and roots. Next, you can proceed to the edibility test if there is no reaction. " It is important to remember that the skin test isn't fool proof, as stinging plants, such as nettles, are also edible and nutritious and might trigger an allergic reaction. Cooking the nettles first is all that is required.

Alternatively, you can test the edibility of your wild food by placing it directly on your tongue without chewing or ingesting it beforehand. You should wait at least eight hours before carrying out this test. Keep the food out of your mouth as soon as you see a reaction to it on your skin.

Wild food can be tested by placing it in your mouth on the tongue without chewing or swallowing as an alternative method. This test should only be performed a minimum of eight hours after skin-to-skin contact. Do not eat the food if you notice a response on your skin.

Tips for Successful Foraging

1. Be aware of your food and the plant it comes from. The plant should be avoided if you don't know what it is. Many edible plants can be mistaken for toxic ones. Photos of the entire plant and its sections can help you determine whether or not this is the plant you are looking for later.

2. When you're out foraging, have a reference book on edible plants nearby. If you accidentally swallow a deadly plant while you're out alone, having this information handy will help the person who discovers you identify the plant that caused the adverse reaction.

3. The more you practice, the better you get. Before beginning, work with an expert forager or a guide to learn how to recognise and eat these plants.

4. Even if they are going to be boiled or cooked, wild plants still need to be cleaned before consumption. You could become sick if you don't wash the plant first. To remove poisons from larger plants and roots that will not be peeled before cooking or eating raw, perform this procedure.

5. Rather than searching for food on a long hike or foraging adventure, bring a lunch. After lunch, you'll be able to forage for edible plants along the trail and start your journey with more energy.

6. When consuming plants, you don't know, be cautious. If you follow the letter's instructions, your body may still react negatively to the plant.

7. If you're with someone else, you can test how your body reacts by taking turns eating a small piece of the plant.

8. Do not ingest these wild edible plants raw or in large quantities, as some may be harmful.

9. You should always have a first aid kit if someone is allergic to the plant.

10. Eat nothing before consulting with your doctor to be sure it's okay to do so.

In addition to sugars, carbohydrates, and oils, edible plants can be consumed and supply the body with additional nutritional value. Wild and ripe plants, as well as plants that have gone to seed, can be eaten. Since there are several wild edible plants to be found worldwide, a list of these can be discovered at a library or online.

Wild edible plants are great food and medicinal source. However, certain portions of the plant are more nutrient-dense. There are many edible parts to this herb that you can utilise to maximise your nutritional intake.

If you prepare edible plants appropriately, you can eat them without fear for your health. To avoid poisoning yourself, it is crucial to know which wild edible plants are safe. It's wise to avoid the plant if you have no idea what it is. Unless you're well-versed in plant nutrition and have a doctor's nod, you should avoid consuming any plants.

When and How to Harvest

Before you even consider harvesting a plant, you must first identify it. Please don't take a chance with wild plants; they can be deadly. Before you begin harvesting plants, keep these points in mind.

Season

Most wild plants are seasonal, meaning they are only available for a limited time each year. Perennial plants, on the other hand, can be picked all year round. Keeping a foraging journal will help you identify which plants thrive in your area over the several seasons, including winter, spring, fall, and summer. On the other hand, other plants should be picked as soon as possible since they become inedible after a certain point of growth. Before harvesting, some plants need to reach a certain maturity stage. As a result, you must thoroughly understand the many stages of growth and life cycles of plants.

Method of Harvesting

You can improve your harvesting abilities if you are familiar with a plant's life cycle. It's possible to harvest wild plants in various ways, like picking the leaves and flowers, cutting the stems, or digging out the roots. You should be able to identify when a plant is ready to be harvested based on certain signs. The fading of leaves, for example, signifies the readiness for harvesting fruits or edible roots.

It is necessary to analyse the entire plant when harvesting it. Verify the health of the plant's leaves, roots, seeds, and flowers. A plant's colour should be consistent with that of its species. Some more fragile plants, such as young ones, are delicious. The thin fibrous skin must be peeled off before eating. As the plants mature, they will harden, become more fibrous, and become more pliable. Some plants can move from being delicious to rancid if they aren't picked in time.

Harvesting aromatic flowers are best done in the early morning on a dry day when the flowers have not yet fully opened. As a result, these plants' medicinal value and potency will be preserved to their full potential. In addition, the type of plant (woody or herbaceous), the time of year, and the plant component you wish to collect can influence the method you use to harvest plants. The removal of any mouldy, damaged, discoloured, or blackened portions should also be a priority for you.

Exercise Safe Harvesting

When harvesting, be careful not to damage the delicate leaves of the plants. Please ensure you ethically gather the plants so future generations can use them. When gathering leaves or other plant components from the wild, it is essential to use sustainable methods. If you want to use the edible sections of the plant, don't remove the whole thing. Don't harm the branches if you wish to use leaves. If you gather the leaves correctly, you can return to the same plant multiple times throughout the year.

The plant's latent buds below will generate more leaves faster if you pinch out the growing tips just above the node. Spring salads are best served with soft, fresh baby leaves. Never, ever remove all of the leaves from a plant. Due to the absence of transpiration through the leaves, this can damage it. The plant can also be affected by pests and diseases. It is also possible for plants without leaves to seed early, which could have long-term consequences for the species.

Harvesting Stems from Edible Wild Plants

When harvesting edible plant stems, use sharp secateurs, a pruning saw, or a knife. Allow the buds to sprout by cutting above the node if possible. In addition, this prevents a dead stem from decaying and spreading disease to the rest of the plant. The entire plant should be harvested before flowering and at ground level whenever possible. You can use a fork and shake the roots to carefully remove them.

It would help if you properly harvested herbaceous perennial plants so the yield can continue to develop. After you've collected the appropriate components, check to see if the plant can regenerate. When you start with huge branches, the knub should be a few millimetres above the flush. As a result, the buds will be able to continue expanding.

How to Gather Fruits

It would be best if you kept in mind that not every wild fruit is in its freshest and most luscious form. Some wild fruits are ready to be harvested when they are still wet, while others dry up before they can be harvested. Seed pods from some plants contain edible seeds and nuts, while those from other plants are dry and inedible. Certain species have edible tenders at the beginning. Some of the pods will explode, causing them to disperse randomly. You can gather these while they're still linked to the parent plant or when they drop to the ground.

Depending on how you intend to utilize the pods, you can harvest them while they are fresh. In rare situations, the pods can be harvested when they turn yellow. Dry fruits can be picked and shelled by hand. When you're done shelling the dried pods, ensure the seeds aren't damaged, and then winnow the chaff.

Fresh, juicy, and frequently adaptable seed pods from other wild plants can be picked at any time of the year and used in many ways. Fleshy fruits should be harvested when they are just about to burst open. Many products, such as sauces and jams, are made from these fruits. Fruits of other varieties should be gathered as soon as they are ready. You can determine when a fruit is ripe by its colour, which is true for most fruits.

Several plants, such as elderberries and rowans, must be chopped in half. You'll have to do the stripping yourself home, so only the bare essentials will remain. When ripe, blackberries and raspberries pop right off your fingertips. You must be careful when handling these delicate fruits. Because they are the size of apples, hawthorns are easy to remove by gently twisting them with your fingers. Keep your hands off the new growth spurs likely to generate flowers and buds for the upcoming year. There is no need to exert effort when harvesting hawthorns when they are ripe.

Place a plastic bag over ripe seed heads to collect them and gather seeds or pods. Nuts can either be left in the bag for a few days or shook for quick harvesting if you want. Another option is to cut the stems and hang the plants upside down in a designated area of your home. Alternatively, Seeds will begin to fall after a few days if you leave them alone. Make sure you have a designated area for the nuts to gather.

Harvesting Bark and Roots

Barks and roots can also be harvested from edible wild plants. You can use these to your advantage when you're stranded in the wilderness. Spring is the best time to harvest bark since sap levels are at their highest. If the plant is soft, it will be easier to peel away. Other kinds of bark, however, can be gathered at any time of year. Because no additional equipment is needed, gathering bark is a simple process. A cutter is all you need to create a cut. The sap-pumping vascular system of most plants is found in the inner bark, which is why it is so important in herbal medicine.

When collecting bark, it would be best to not disturb the xylem and phloem cells in the cambium layer of cells. The xylem cells connect the plant's roots to the rest of the plant. Phloem cells, on the other hand, connect the plant's leaves to its roots. As the cambium layer of cells regenerates in woody plants, the plant's potential to expand is bolstered by this process. Additionally, there are cambium cells along the central portion of the tree's trunk or branch. There are numerous components in soft bark that you will remove when harvesting it. The inner bark can be readily peeled away from the rest of the plant when harvested in the spring. Do it slowly, and you'll see it's a simple process. The plant can produce new bark if it's handled correctly.

Roots are listed in various herbal medicine books, and depending on the plant you want to harvest, they can also be utilized as food. Autumn or spring is the finest time to gather roots. Since the plants can take sugars and other nutrients before returning to dormancy in the fall, harvesting perennial roots at this time is best for your region. At this point, the roots are loaded with medicinal compounds and have reached their peak of nutritional content. During the spring, the plants will begin to consume their nutrients after a long winter of rest.

On the other hand, winter frosts would have affected roots collected in the winter. Carbohydrates are converted to simple sugars in these enzymes, resulting in a more flavourful product. When harvesting the roots of biennial plants, it's ideal to do so at the end of the first year. Using the right Digging tools is crucial for harvesting roots. Harvesting tap-rooted plants, for example, will necessitate extensive digging and force. Digging carefully is essential to get the root out in one piece.

Make a broad circle around the plant's base before harvesting fibrous-rooted plants. The roots can be shaken loose by removing a clod from the area around the circle's perimeter. To keep the plant in place, you can pluck the roots out of the ground as you excavate. Fill the holes around the plant with soil and place the roots in a bag. If you decide to remove the entire plant, be careful to replace it with a new one to ensure its long-term viability.

Harvesting Grass

Grass contains many nutrients and medicinal compounds that can benefit your health. You'll need a pair of scissors and a bag to collect them. Put the edible components you intend to consume in a carrier bag after carefully removing them. The grass you intend to eat should be in good condition.

Our ancestors have relied on foraging for survival since the dawn of mankind. People are becoming increasingly interested in foraging for wild edible foods since it is an excellent way to obtain nutrients and maintain a sense of connection to the land. It can also be done as a hobby. This chapter has given you an overview of what you need to know before you begin. Always prioritize your safety and avoid potentially hazardous fruits and plants. The best way to learn about new species is to take a test on the one you're unfamiliar with. To gather wild edibles, you might employ a variety of techniques. The fruits and seeds should only be harvested when they are ripe and ready.

Your Tools and Equipment

The tools you need to dig, saw, chop, and clip plants are probably already in your garden shed or kitchen. It may be necessary to trek across isolated wilderness areas to find edible wild plants. It would be impossible to hike through the woods with a standard set of gardening tools. The greatest tools for foraging can be carried easily and aren't heavy.

Here are essentials that no aspiring forager should attempt to acquire before venturing into the wild. Foraging will be safer, more pleasurable, and more productive with the help of these products. The following items can be purchased in outdoor or survival retail stores or online.

1. **Shears and Scissors:** Pruning shears and kitchen scissors are important if you can only afford to buy two items to get started. Minimal effort is required to use a pruning shear to cut stems, twigs, small branches, and roots in small places.

   Cleavers, chickweed, and violet have tender young stems, making a pair of kitchen scissors a great instrument for harvesting them. To pick delicate greens, pruning shears' blades are too short and unwieldy. It's best to get pruning shears from a company that makes replacement parts, such as springs, easily accessible.

2. **Shovel:** Foragers use shovels to remove burdock and other tap-rooted plants from compact soil. Rather than a flat and straight-edged spade, seek a folding shovel with a pointed concave blade. A long shovel handle will provide you more leverage than a small handle, which is less effective.

   Perfect are multi-purpose shovels with extendable handles. Examples are Kepeak, Sirius, and Kopwin, which all have headlocks at 90 degrees for hoes. It is possible that you won't use all the extras that come with these survival gear, such as a compass, fire starters, screwdrivers, bottle openers, etc.

Shallow root plants like leeks, cattail, Indian cucumber, and wild potato are best removed with a small hand shovel or trowel that may fit in a pocket. Folding hand shovels made entirely of steel, such as the U-Dig-It, are an excellent example. Some foragers of wild plants prefer digging roots using a typical garden fork. It's because the tines of a fork are less prone to damaging roots than a shovel or spade. In the field, however, they are unusable due to their bulk and inability to be carried easily.

To loosen the dirt around root plants in harder soil, you may always bring a solid knife and whittle a pointed digging stick. Depending on how often you want to forage and how much you're ready to pay to make your pack light and manageable, you should select a digging and extracting tool accordingly.

3. **Saw:** When collecting medicinal tree bark such as black birch and wild cherry, a pruning saw comes in handy. Cutting small to medium-sized tree branches is a pleasure with this instrument. Most garden centres carry folding pruning saws.

   Knives and saws can be attached to multi-function shovels, as described above in the shovel section, saving the user from carrying around additional tools.

4. **Knife:** For cutting stems and vines, pruning knives are the ideal tool. The hawkbill blade's hook design makes it perfect for cutting through ground-level vegetation. Pruning knives with non-slip handles and a foldaway blade with a lock-back clip are recommended. A clip-on belt handle makes it easy to carry and accessible while foraging for wild plants.

   The Japanese hori-hori weeding and digging knife is another built-for-purpose knife that some foragers like. On one side, the blades are sharp and straight; on the other, they're serrated, making these knives non-folding. Some foragers claim that wooden handles are more durable than plastic ones. A leather sheath can be attached to a belt to carry the weapon comfortably. To avoid cutting your hand, look for models with a guard between the handle and the blade.

5. **Gloves:** When foraging, it's best to carry two sets of gloves: one set of thin gloves and another set of heavier, more durable gloves. When picking

berries, you'll want a pair of thin and flexible gloves. Leather or canvas gloves are ideal for protecting your hands when needed.

A pair of long-sleeved gauntlet gloves made of cowhide is great for foraging in thorny shrubs, such as roses. Plants can cause a painful skin reaction with fine hairs and thorns, such as those in the wild.

6. **Brush:** Remove as much soil as possible from the root harvests before placing them in your foraging bag. This job requires a stiff-bristled brush.

7. **Containers:** Foraging for wild plants necessitates the use of a container large enough to hold your haul and keep it as fresh as possible on the way home.

8. **Bags:** Since plastic bags restrict ventilation, retain moisture, and cause plants to wither and disintegrate quickly, they should not be used. Reusable bags made of hemp, linen, or brown paper are available at most supermarkets. These can be folded flat and put under your wild plant field guide books because they have handles. For fashion-conscious foragers, there are bags specifically designed for plant foraging.

9. **Baskets:** Woven baskets are a common mode of transporting plants for some foragers. Having handles or backpack straps makes it easier to carry heavy weight, while its open weave construction aids in airflow. Herbs can be air-dried at home in wide, flat baskets.

10. **Buckets:** When transporting your wild plant collection, you'll need a variety of three and five-gallon food-grade buckets. Use these to transport heavy harvests like elderberries or wild blueberries that you can't carry in the trunk of your car. Use some water to keep the produce fresh while it's being transported back to your home.

11. **Magnifying Glass:** A magnifying glass is a must-have item for identifying edible plant species when out foraging. Choose one with a magnification of between 10 and 30 times. Using a jeweller's loupe magnifier is the ideal option because it's small and lightweight. Many additionally include a built-in LED light that can be used to illuminate the subject at hand.

12. **Flashlight:** Having a flashlight in your bag is a good idea, too. A torch may be necessary if you're foraging under a forest canopy at dusk. In the event of

an emergency, you'll want to have access to a cell phone. Never go foraging without a flashlight and some extra batteries.

13. **First Aid Bag:** Minor cuts, abrasions, and thorn penetration of exposed hands and forearms are inevitable when foraging for edible wild plants. You can't go on a field trip without one of them. Plasters, disinfectants, antihistamine cream, and tweezers should be included.

You'll learn more about the healing benefits of wild plants as you gain proficiency in recognizing them. Your first aid kit should include herbal ointments from the collected wild plants.

14. **Water:** It would be best to have a water bottle or hydration bag handy when you're out in the field. Foraging edible wild plants can be physically taxing, depending on the region and terrain. Getting dehydrated in a remote area can be dangerous.

15. **Field Guide Book or Plant ID App:** A wild plant identification app or field guidebook is one of the essential items in your foraging gear. When it comes to foraging, knowing which plants won't harm you and which ones can't.

Universal Edibility Test

Plant Edibility Testing is a survival field guide developed by the US Army to assist soldiers in identifying edible plants and avoiding dangerous species in remote areas.

The test can be found as part of the Army Techniques Publication (2018, ATP 3-50.2). Foragers, hikers, and outdoor lovers are often taught survival skills, using it as a reference for universal edibility assessment by the private sector. To help soldiers survive while foraging for food in unfamiliar areas, the relevant section of the paper has been summarised here. As a result, they may not be applicable in the United States.

Step	Wait Time
Fast	8 hours
Smell Test	N/A
Visual Test	N/A
Skin Test	N/A
Lip Test	8 minutes
Taste Test	8 minutes
Swallow Test	16 hours
Quantity Test	N/A

Step-by-Step Guide

Do not consume anything for at least eight hours before taking the exam. Because of this, you can be confident any health problems you may have been caused by the plant and not something else you've consumed. It will take 24 hours for this test to be completed.

Step 1: Examine the smell for yourself; the smell of mould or mustiness could suggest that the plant is not edible. The plant should be thrown away if it emits an almond aroma.

Step 2: Observational Test Determine the colour of the plant's sap by crushing or breaking a portion. Step two is to check whether the sap is clear before moving on.

Step 3: Skin Reaction Testing On your inner forearm, apply a drop of juice or sap from the plant. Observe the skin for irritation, including a rash or tingling sensation. Otherwise, continue with the rest of the process.

Step 4: Lip Reaction Test, A drop or smear of the plant juice can be applied on the outer lip for eight minutes if the inner forearm does not react. If you see a reaction, stop the test and see if it goes away.

Step 5: Taste Reaction Test; for eight minutes, taste a small piece of the plant with your tongue, and don't chew it if you don't have any reaction. Please stop the test immediately if the taste is unpleasant. Such as bitterness or the sensation of the tongue being paralyzed. Swallow the plant fragment if no reaction occurs.

Step 6: Swallow Reaction Test; once you've swallowed, wait for eight hours. If it doesn't work, try swallowing some plants after chewing on them for a few seconds. Wait a full eight hours before trying again. Consider the plant portion tested edible if there is no adverse reaction.

Step 7: Quantity Tolerance Test, Consume small amounts of the plant at a time. Make it a habit for your body to adjust to it. Consuming huge amounts of the plant could be dangerous.

Caution Note

Make sure that every portion of the plant may be eaten. It's possible to eat sections of some plants that are both edible and poisonous. The same holds when it comes to raw plants. Different people may have different sensitivities to the same plant. Fasting might cause diarrhoea, nausea, or cramps if you eat large amounts of plant substances on an empty stomach.

As a general rule, stay away from unidentified or wild plants that exhibit the following characteristics:

1. Black, pink, or purple coloured grain head spurs
2. Discoloured, milky sap (juice) in the roots, stems, or leaves
3. Foliage that looks like a carrot, dill, parsnip, or parsley
4. Plants that have three-leafed growth patterns
5. Pods containing beans, bulbs, or seeds
6. Soapy or bitter taste.
7. Thorns, spines, or fine hairs
8. Woody parts and leaves that have an almond scent

When selecting edible wild plants, these eight characteristics should be employed as a sort of weeding out process. You can use the universal edibility test to prevent eating or even touching plants that may be harmful.

Global Edible Wild Plants

A wide variety of these ten plants may be found in nearly every biome and are safe to eat raw or cooked:

1. Aggregate berries
2. Cattail
3. Clover
4. Dandelion
5. Fiddlehead fern
6. Onions
7. Plantain
8. Segmented grass
9. Thistle
10. Wild rosehip

Most Common Global Plants to Procure:

Cattail: The starch content in rhizomes (underground stems) is particularly high. They can be purchased all year long. After removing the spongy surrounding tissue, the starchy core can be chewed and consumed raw. Boiling the rhizome makes it safe to consume in its entirety. In the spring and early summer, the isolated individual can eat green shoots, green blossoms, golden pollen, and the white inner leaves of immature stems.

Ferns: There are more than 10,000 different kinds of ferns in the world. Only a few of them are deemed moderately hazardous. Fiddleheads, the young, unrolling fern fronds, look like the end of a violin. It's possible to eat fiddleheads raw, but they're better cooked. Using ferns to eliminate worms in the digestive and intestinal tracts is possible.

Bamboo: There are over 1,200 species of bamboo globally. They are the largest of all grasses. Young shoots (rhizomes) are edible and have the most nutritional value.

Palms: Climates across temperate, arid, and tropical regions are home to 2,600 palm species. Succulent starch and sugar can be found in the palm heart, where the plant's leaves grow. Coconuts, dates, and other palm fruits are safe to eat.

In addition, the following plants are safe sources of food:

- Acacia (Acacia farnesiana)
- Agave (Agave species)
- Amaranth (Amaranths retroflex and other species)
- Arrowroot (Sagittarius species)
- Asparagus (Asparagus officials)
- Bamboo (Ambusa and other species)
- Bananas (Musa species)
- Beechnut (Fags species)
- Blackberries (Rube's species)
- Blueberries (Vaccinium species)
- Breadfruit (Artocarpus incisa)
- Burdock (Arctium lappa)
- Cactus (various species)
- Cashew (Anacardium occidental)
- Coconut (Cocoa nucifera)
- Chestnut (Castanea species)
- Chicory (Cichorium intybus)
- Chufa (Cyperus esculentus)
- Date palm (Phoenix dactylifera)
- Daylily (Hemerocallis fulva)
- Desert amaranth (Amaranths palmer)
- Mango (Mangifera indica)
- Nettle (Urtica species)

- Oaks (Quercus species)
- Palms (various species)
- Papaya (Carica species)
- Persimmon (Diospyros virginiana)
- Pokeweed (Phytolacca americana)
- Prickly pear cactus (Opuntia species)
- Purslane (Portulaca oleracea)
- Sassafras (Sassafras albidum)
- Sheep sorrel (Rumex acetosella)
- Strawberries (Fragaria species)
- Sugarcane (Saccharum officinarum)
- Taro (Colocasia species)
- Water lily and lotus (Nuphar, Nelumbo, and other species)
- Wild onion and garlic (Allium species)
- Wild rose (Rosa species)
- Wood sorrel (Oxalis species)

Warning

Wild mushrooms and fungus should not be eaten since they contain toxins. Many fungi contain poisonous peptides, which are protein-based poisons. Mushrooms can be dangerous or safe to eat, although this is not always easy to establish. Moreover, they are a poor source of nourishment.

Wild Plant Nutritional Information

In addition to providing a source of energy, the nutritional value of the meals we eat is critical to the proper functioning of our bodies and the efficient transfer of energy. A well-balanced diet rich in all nutrients is essential to avoid deficiency or hormonal imbalances. Additionally, a healthy diet might aid in the fight against viral infections and other disorders. Using the following tables, you may calculate your daily recommended intake of various nutrients.

Dandelion:

Dandelion greens offer 45 calories of food energy which are high in vitamins A and C, as well as iron, calcium, and manganese, in a 100-gram serving (3.5 ounces).

Nutritional value per 100 g (3.5 oz) serving:		
	%DV†	**Quantity**
Energy	-%	45 calories
Carbohydrates	3 %	9.2 g
Sugars	-%	0.71 g
Dietary fibre	13 %	3.5 g
Fat	1 %	0.7 g
Protein	-%	2.7 g
Vitamins		
Vitamin A	64%	508 µg
beta-Carotene	54%	5,854 µg
lutein zeaxanthin	-%	13,610 µg
Thiamine (B1)	17	0.19 mg

Riboflavin (B2)	%	0.26 mg
Niacin (B3)	22%	0.806 mg
Pantothenic acid (B5)	5%	0.084 mg
Vitamin B6	2%	0.251 mg
Folate (B9)	19%	27 µg
Choline	7%	35.3 µg
Vitamin C	42%	35 mg
Vitamin E	23%	3.44 mg
Vitamin K	741%	778.4 µg

Minerals

Calcium	14%	187 mg
Iron	17%	3.1 mg
Magnesium	10%	36 mg
Manganese	16%	0.342 mg
Phosphorus	9%	66 mg
Potassium	8%	397 mg
Sodium	5%	76 mg
Zinc	4%	0.41 mg
Other: Water		85.6 g

Note:

Units: µg = micrograms • mg = milligrams • IU = International units.

†Percentages are roughly approximated using US recommendations for adults.

Blackberries:

Raw blackberries, in a serving of 100 g (3.5 ounces), provide 43 calories and 5 grams of dietary fibre, or 25% of the Daily Value (DV). Vitamin C and vitamin K make up 25% and 19% of the daily value (DV) in 100 grams, respectively, whereas the nutrient content of other essentials is low.

Nutritional value per 100 g (3.5 oz) serving:		
	%DV†	**Quantity**
Energy	-%	45 calories
Carbohydrates	3 %	9.2 g
Sugars	-%	0.71 g
Dietary fibre	20 %	3.5 g
Fat	- %	0.7 g
Protein	2%	2.7 g
Vitamins		
Vitamin A	214 IU	
Thiamine (B1)	2%	0.020 mg
Riboflavin (B2)	2%	0.026 mg
Niacin (B3)	4%	0.646 mg
Vitamin B6	2%	0.030 mg
Folate (B9)	6%	25 µg
Vitamin C	25%	21.0 mg
Vitamin E	8%	1.17 mg

Vitamin K	19%	19.8 µg
Minerals		
Calcium	3%	29 mg
Iron	5%	0.62 mg
Magnesium	6%	20 mg
Phosphorus	3%	22 mg
Potassium	3%	162 mg
Sodium	-%	1 mg
Zinc	6%	0.53 mg

Note:

Units: µg = micrograms • mg = milligrams • IU = International units.

†Percentages are roughly approximated using US recommendations for adults.

Radish:

Raw radishes have 16 calories per three-and-a-half-ounce serving, according to the USDA. A low concentration of other necessary nutrients is accompanied by a modest intake of vitamin C (18% of the DV) (refer to table). Raw radish is 95% water, 3% carbohydrate, 1% protein, and has very little amounts of lipids.

Nutritional value per 100 g (3.5 oz) serving:		
	%DV†	Quantity
Energy	-%	16 calories
Carbohydrates	-%	3.4 g
Sugars	-%	1.86 g
Dietary fibre	-%	1.6 g
Fat	-%	0.1 g
Protein	-%	0.68 g
Vitamins		
Thiamine (B1)	1%	0.012 mg
Riboflavin (B2)	3%	0.039 mg
Niacin (B3)	2%	0.254 mg
Pantothenic acid (B5)	3%	0.165 mg
Vitamin B6	5%	0.071 mg
Folate (B9)	6%	25 µg
Vitamin C	18%	14.8 mg
Minerals		

Calcium	3%	25 mg
Iron	3%	0.34 mg
Magnesium	3%	10 mg
Manganese	3%	0.069 mg
Phosphorus	3%	20 mg
Potassium	3%	233 mg
Zinc	3%	0.28 mg
Other		
Water		95.3 g

Note:

Units: µg = micrograms • mg = milligrams • IU = International units.

†Percentages are roughly approximated using US recommendations for adults.

Seaweed Gelatine:

Gracilaria and Gelidium are red algal species commonly used to make agar, sometimes known as "agar-agar" (botanical division Rhodophyta). The melting point of gelatine and agar is one of the key variances between the two (the point at which the gel returns to liquid form). There is a difference in melting points between gelatine and agar gel. As a result, agar can be used in hot regions without refrigeration. There are 306 calories in one serving of dried agar seaweed in one hundred ounces. Calcium, iron, magnesium, and potassium are all abundant in agar, making it an excellent food source for those needing it.

Nutritional value per 100 g (3.5 oz) serving:		
	%DV†	Quantity
Carbohydrates	27%	81 g
Dietary fibre	32%	8 g
Protein	12%	6 g
Minerals		
Calcium	62%	- mg
Iron	118%	- mg
Magnesium	192%	- mg
Sodium	32%	1,125 mg

Note:

Units: µg = micrograms • mg = milligrams • IU = International units.

†Percentages are roughly approximated using US recommendations for adults.

Wild Rice:

Gluten-free wild rice has a similar protein content to genuine rice and is only second to oats in terms of protein content. Wild rice is particularly abundant in the amino acid lysine and its high protein content. It is a good source of nutritional fibre and is low in calories. Cooked wild rice delivers 5 percent more iron, potassium, riboflavin, and thiamine than commercially cultivated rice; 10 percent more folate, magnesium, niacin, phosphorus, and vitamin B6; 15 percent more zinc; and more than 20 percent more manganese than commercially grown rice.

Nutritional value per 100 g (3.5 oz) serving:		
	%DV†	**Quantity**
Energy	-%	101 calories
Carbohydrates	-%	21.34 g
Dietary fibre	-%	1.8 g
Fat	-%	0.34 g
Protein	-%	3.99 g
Vitamins		
Vitamin A	-%	64 µg
Thiamine (B1)	5 %	0.052 mg
Riboflavin (B2)	7 %	0.087 mg
Niacin (B3)	9 %	1.287 mg
Vitamin B6	10 %	0.135 mg
Folate (B9)	7 %	26 µg
Vitamin E	2 %	0.24 mg

Minerals

Calcium	-%	187 mg
Copper	6 %	
Iron	5 %	3.1 mg
Magnesium	9 %	36 mg
Manganese	13 %	0.342 mg
Phosphorus	12 %	66 mg
Potassium	2 %	397 mg
Sodium	-%	76 mg
Zinc	14 %	0.41 mg

Note:

Units: µg = micrograms • mg = milligrams • IU = International units.

†Percentages are roughly approximated using US recommendations for adults.

Plantain:

Raw plantain leaves offer 122 calories per half-cup portion (approximately 3.5 oz/100g). This food's amount of vitamin C is moderately high (30% of the RDV), but the other nutrients are scarce.

Nutritional value per 100 g (3.5 oz) serving:		
	%DV†	**Quantity**
Energy	-%	122 calories
Carbohydrates	10 %	22 g
Sugars	-%	15 g
Dietary fibre	9 %	2.3 g
Fat	-%	0.4 g
Protein	2 %	1.3 g
Vitamins		
Vitamin B6	15%	- mg
Vitamin C	30%	18 mg
Minerals		
Iron	3 %	- mg
Magnesium	9 %	36 mg
Potassium	14 %	499 mg
Sodium	- %	4 mg

Note:

Units: µg = micrograms • mg = milligrams • IU = International units.

†Percentages are roughly approximated using US recommendations for adults.

Preserving Wild Edible Plants

The wonderful thing about wild edible plants is that they can provide you with a lot of nutrition. This nutrition comes at almost no cost, and if you eat a diet composed of these wild plants, you'll be able to get more nutrients than you get with your regular store-bought diet. However, the main issue with wild plants is availability.

When you harvest the wild plants, they immediately start degenerating, and if you don't preserve them soon enough, you'll be unable to use them for long. Most of these wild edible plants grow edible parts only during the summer, and if you live in an area where the winter's harsh, you'll have a very short window to preserve your food. You must understand the proper preservation techniques if you want to store these edibles for later use.

Another thing that you should remember is that the storage technique has to be right, or else the food you store may rot or develop harmful fungus. There are a variety of preservation techniques that you can employ to preserve these foods safely. We'll be looking at all the different preservation methods that you can use to store the edible plants for future use without any chances of spoiling them.

We'll also look at how these stored foods can be transported to maintain their freshness and ensure no losses occur. You may need to travel from one place to another, leading to unnecessary spoilage. You may not have access to a refrigerator or preservatives, which can increase the odds of your food getting spoiled. The section on transportation will explain the proper transportation methods and the precautions you should take.

Even though you might have tried your best to preserve these edible foods, some of them will inevitably go bad. It's an important aspect of storing these plants that cannot be avoided. However, you should know when these plants have gone bad so that you don't consume anything that may be harmful to your health. We'll briefly discuss how you can spot edibles that have gone bad to the point of no return. This way, you can learn how to avoid any health hazards and only consume the edible plants that are still consumable.

Preservation Methods

A variety of preservation methods can be used that do not require much high-tech equipment to keep your plants consumable for a long time. Whatever you choose will depend on each method's different pros and cons. Ensure you properly clean all the wild harvest you have collected. Properly rinse it after soaking it for a while. Soaking is a very important step as it can help you clean off any dirt or debris from your wild edibles, and it can also help to reinvigorate the greens and keep them fresh. The wild plants stored this way will be tastier and fresher when you start preserving them.

While some methods are fairly low-tech and easy to do, others may require a bit more effort on your end. So, let's find out methods you can use to enjoy the fruits or plants of your harvest for a long time.

Drying

The age-old drying out of the plants to remove moisture is one of the most efficient preservation methods. Even when using this method, you can go for the top-notch options by utilizing electric dehydrators or use some ingenious solutions to do it cheaply. The electric dehydrators can eliminate almost all of the moisture from your food, but they don't come cheap and can get very expensive.

Another option that you can opt for is a solar drying box. These boxes will save you a lot of electricity and will be cheaper in the long run but will cost you a lot initially. However, these solar drying boxes can be built at home if you're even little experienced in building things yourself. Building one will save you a large chunk of money you'd otherwise spend buying a factory-made unit.

Another way to dry out your edible plants is to use the sun's natural energy. This free option will do its job nicely, considering the price you pay for it. Just try to keep your edible plants out in the sun until they don't change their color anymore. Once the color has changed, you can remove them from the sunlight, which will last you a long time. To expedite this process faster, you can try to slice the edible plant into smaller pieces and apply a little lemon juice before you place it under the sunlight. This will ensure that the edibles dry out faster and don't attract any microbes.

Most dried-out weeds and herbs can be ground into powdered forms, which will help you keep away any moisture by packing it in an airtight container. Anytime you need to use these materials, you can rehydrate them or blend them with oil to be used as dressings or chutneys.

This method works out great with almost all fruit and vegetables. If you have a fleshier vegetable or fruit, you can sprinkle a bit of salt on it, resulting in much better dehydration. You'll find the best results when drying out leafy vegetables with more surface area, and the fruit will remain leathery even after they dry out.

Pickling

Another great method to preserve your wild edibles is to pickle them in a brine of salt or vinegar. You can choose either option depending on the flavor and aroma you desire. It's a very simple and effective way to preserve vegetables because of the ample availability of both these ingredients. Just try to do it in a sterile environment for the best results. If you fail to eliminate any unwanted bacteria from your containers or water, it'll result in a pickle that tastes weird and smells funny.

If you go through the entire process correctly, you'll achieve preservation that enhances the taste of the bland food and is very beneficial to your health. You'll need to keep your pickle refrigerated for its longevity, and when properly kept, it can last as long as 6 weeks. A good pickle will keep your gut populated with good bacteria, and you'll also be able to digest the foods better.

Many people choose to add additional ingredients like garlic, ginger, clove, or dried chili peppers. These additions give your pickle a complex taste that will increase the variety of your palette. You can preserve almost any wild plant like chickweed leaves, plantain, or dandelions this way, and it'll most likely still taste good.

Blanching and Freezing:

Blanching is a very simple process in which you must put your vegetables in scalding water or under steam for a short period. This has many benefits for your health because it cleans the surface and kills any microorganisms on the vegetable skin. The other very useful benefits are the enhancement in colour, the slowed loss of vitamins and minerals, and the softening of the vegetable, making it easier to store.

After you're done blanching, all you need to do is put the food in the freezer. Once the food is frozen, you can pack all of it into plastic bags that can be used very conveniently. You can take out a packet whenever you need it and thaw it before using the vegetables for cooking. It's highly advised that you don't re-freeze your food once you thaw it as it can lead to losing the quality of your vegetables.

Even though frozen food can't be used in a salad, it can be used to cook other nutritious food. Refrigeration technology has become cheaper and more effective than any limited energy source like solar energy. It's a time-tested method for preserving vegetables and is your best bet if you want to preserve your vegetables' taste and quality for a long time.

Unlike other methods, you can preserve your vegetables for a long time, which can barely last a month to a season. Frozen veggies are fresh up to 8 to 10 months after being packed, and that's plenty of time for you to grow a new harvest. Try to refrigerate your vegetables as much as possible because this is rather easy and longer-lasting.

Transporting Wild Edible Plants

Procuring and preserving wild edible plants is all fine until you're forced to transport them. You have to be conscious of the pace at which you transport your edibles because that will influence the condition in which it arrives. It might seem like a simple task from the outside, but it takes a lot of effort to achieve the desired results.

If you want to ensure that your preserved edibles don't get spoiled, it's a good idea to clean up the transportation space. If you can't keep the surroundings clean, it may lead to contamination 0f your preserved foods, which will eventually lead to spoilage of the entire crop. Cleaning your transportation is one of the most straightforward ways to ensure safer transportation and can be easily completed in less than an hour.

Another important aspect you must remember is the temperature at which you store your wild edible plants. All the wild edible plants require different temperatures to be stored, and you must keep this consideration in mind. It's also very important to maintain and constantly regulate the temperature to ensure that there is no deterioration of the quality of edibles. You can purchase a refrigerator or hire a refrigerated truck to provide the best cooling options. If you choose to purchase a mini-fridge or cool box, it'll be an investment that will be well worth it in the future.

The shelf life of the preserved edible plants is another factor that should be kept in mind while transporting. If you can't keep the preserved edibles refrigerated, then it becomes more important to consider the shelf life of each product. The shelf life of different plants can vary by a huge margin, and you have to know every plant's durability to better transport them to remote locations. Fresher edibles will always be better than a plant that has wilted away. Fresh plants will retain more of their nutrients over a longer period compared to edibles that have been out in the open without any preservation.

Another thing that you should keep in mind is the seasonality of the wild plants that you harvest. If you can transport the plants in the harvest season, you'll have much better results because the plants will be fresher. Different plants have different growing seasons, and if you're well-acquainted with the entire schedule, you'll be able to harvest, preserve, and transport them more efficiently.

Little mistakes like improper packaging can be a huge issue as well. If you don't stuff enough packaging material into your shipment, it'll lead to the breakage of the containers, which will lead to huge losses. Also, ensure you package your containers tightly and seal them correctly so you don't face any unexpected leakage. If you can avoid these basic mistakes, you'll be able to save a lot of money that would've otherwise been wasted. The advice that safety is better than cure applies perfectly in this situation.

You may face many issues along the way that you didn't even expect. However, if you're prepared well in advance, you'll be able to avoid the associated risks. Later on, the issues that may pop up can be delays, spillage, spoilage, and much more. If you can take proper precautions before transporting the preserved plants, you can avoid unnecessary trouble later on.

Popular Edible Wild Plants In UK & US

There are a wide variety of wild edibles that can be found all over the world. Many plants have cultural significance and can represent various ideas across various cultures. Listed here are some of the most commonly eaten wild edible plants in the UK and US regions.

Dandelion:

In the United States, dandelions are often viewed as a nuisance plant; they are viewed as harmful because they spread over lawns and grow in the area where we have to grow our vegetables or flowers. However, it is used for medicinal purposes, tea, and wine. They have high concentrations of potassium and Vitamin A. A feature that makes this plant useful for humans is that it can detoxify our liver and work better.

As a sunflower relative, dandelions feature hairless leaves with toothed edges and bright yellow blooms. This plant's hollow stems and extensive root system are also notable characteristics. This plant's fragile leaves and bright yellow buds, which will soon grow into seeds, should be harvested in the early spring when they are at their tastiest and most nutritious.

Nettles:

Nettles are considered a wild edible that can be found in the woods and near rivers. This plant has been shown to kill off bacteria and virus to help those with leprosy and malaria. Nettles can be used to heal cuts, wounds, sprains, and bruises, or even as an antiseptic agent. It is also used in making a mixture with other plants to use as a toothpaste or chewing gum that should be applied to the teeth before bed.

It can be used in place of kale or spinach in dishes. As the plants mature, they have green-toothed leaves that grow the other way around. Wear gloves when handling the leaves' undersides to avoid stinging your hands. Nettle plants thrive in somewhat shady locations beside riverbanks. When picked young, nettle leaves taste best when eaten raw in salads. While sensitive, they lack the stinging features that come with maturation.

Garlic Mustard:

Garlic mustard is also known as wild garlic. This plant has been used for many years by indigenous people to fight off viruses and bacteria. It can be used in the kitchen for making a tasty salad or as a vegetable that can be eaten raw or cooked. It benefits people with diabetes as it will help control blood sugar levels. Garlic mustard heightens the effects of the spicy flavor in foods while reducing pain, inflammation, and swelling caused by arthritis and joint pain.

Garlic mustard's leaves are deep green and spherical, with scalloped edges and prominent veining. These slender, bushy plants can be found on forest floors in early spring. Identifying garlic mustard is as simple as crushing a few leaves between your palms and inhaling their pungent aroma.

Elderberry:

Elderberries are a popular wild edible in the United States and Great Britain. The plant is easy to recognize, as it produces dark purple berries often made into a jam or pie. It is also used when teething a baby or when the child or adult has a sore throat. Boil some elderberries in water and use it to gargle for relief from sore throats, colds, and fevers. The shrub can be used to create an astringent and make a mouthwash or gargle to treat ulcers, sores, and sore throats because it can kill bacteria by contracting the blood vessels.

The clusters of white flowers with petals that emerge from light green stems are a good indicator of flowering elderberry bushes. In the summer, the clusters of around 20 dark purple berries are apparent, forming an umbrella-like structure. There are numerous ways to use the flowers and berries in your culinary creations, such as making infusions, cordials, wine, and tea. If you want to get the full flavour of the berries, you'll have to wait until they are fully developed.

Wild Raspberry:

Raspberry can be found in woodlands in mountainous regions. They are known for their sweet flavour and can be eaten fresh or dried. It is used to make jellies, jams, and juices. The leaves of the plants are light green with a serrated edge. This plant has an amazing medicinal value as it also has high concentrations of Vitamin C. The bacteria that cause cholera cannot survive in the body's acidic pH levels, which is usually caused by drinking water containing this wild edible plant. This will help the body maintain its pH levels by neutralizing the acidic compounds in our food.

Before eating the berries, wash them first, and you can enjoy them raw if you want to enjoy the most nutritional content. You may also add them to your favourite baking recipes for heightened tartness.

Curled Dock:

Also known as yellow dock, this plant is an alternative to spinach for salads and stir-fries. It is widely used as a traditional medicine in the United Kingdom. Young leaves are also edible and are used widely. Raw, they are very bitter and should be consumed in small doses. They have diuretic properties that flush out toxins from the body and supply minerals such as iron, magnesium, zinc, and potassium.

This yellow-flowered weed will grow up to a foot tall but tends to trail along the ground.

Asparagus:

Asparagus is one of the most popular plants you will likely find flourishing in spring, which is the best time to go foraging for food. They can be found in healthy soil and under the shade of trees or shrubs. Asparagus is eaten fresh, either raw or steamed. Young shoots are delicate and tender and are usually sold in supermarkets. The stalks contain high levels of potassium, copper, manganese, and Vitamin A, while the leaves offer a good source of Vitamin C. Asparagus is nutritious and can help heal wounds. The mineral-rich shoots also support general health and well-being.

Asparagus is a perennial plant that takes up to five years to produce edible stalks. The asparagus plant grows up to 6 feet tall, has small white flowers in the spring, and its edible parts grow above ground. The stalks or stems come from underground stems called rhizomes. Use fresh asparagus immediately since it turns yellow when exposed to the air.

Root Vegetables:

Wild root vegetables like parsnip, salsify, and wild carrots are good sources of dietary fiber. Root vegetables are good for people with arthritis because the plant's dietary fiber acts as a lubricant in the joints and decreases inflammation. These root vegetables can be easily found in the woods, although some may only be found in recently disturbed areas. They can be eaten either raw or cooked.

As a general rule, do not use wild roots as a substitute for fresh produce because they may contain high amounts of natural toxins. Try to cook them or boil them first before eating.

Cattail:

Cattails (Typha latifolia) can be found around the world. They can be found in many habitats like marshes, bogs, and open fields. These plants are a good source of starch, which is high in protein and carbohydrates. They are known for their dark brown rhizome, which is edible and nutritious. They can be eaten raw or boiled. Cattails are also used for medicinal purposes, such as a diuretic and stimulating the body's lymphatic system.

The cattail is a tall, flowering marsh grass that shoots out of soft, brownish-green-hued rhizomes at the top of the plant. These plants have very small white flowers that rise on tall stalks. The base of the stalk has three oval green leaves protruding out.

Common Poisonous Wild Plants

Wild edible plants that aren't toxic have toxic twins. Although they appear similar to their edible relatives, these twin plants are deadly to humans. While the traditional adage "Leaves of three, leave them alone" may suffice as a general caution to youngsters to keep away from dangerous plants, in your quest for edible wild plants, you'll need more information than that to identify the plants to avoid.

Never touch a plant if you're uncertain about it. Make sure you're just consuming plants that you can be assured.

Nightshade:

Eating these little sparkling blackberries is one of the deadliest North American blueberry look-alikes. Toxic alkaloids and other substances are found in berries that have not yet matured. Ripe berries, on the other hand, are safe to eat in moderation.

This weed is known as Eastern black nightshade in all save the western states of the United States. Nightshade is a member of the Solanum genus along with nettles and food crops such as potatoes and tomatoes. As a result, it's common to see it growing alongside these types of plants.

There are three triangular leaves on the stems of the eastern black nightshade that are slightly hairy. Each berry is one-fourth of an inch in diameter and contains between 50 and 100 seeds; the blossoms are white and star-shaped.

Poisonous Berries:

Approximately 90% of the white and yellow berries, and roughly 50% of the reddish berries, are considered poisonous by botanists. The least hazardous berries are darker in colour (blue or black). This isn't always the case, as the following list of toxic berries illustrates. If you're a beginner, it's better to avoid berries that you can't recognize and be mindful of toxic look-alikes.

Monkshood:

This plant, often known as Adam and Eve or the devil's helmet, is one of the most toxic in the United Kingdom. However, it may be native to moist woodland, meadow, and ditch areas in the southern half of the UK. It is widely naturalised. Known for its beautiful hooded blue flowers, it is a common garden plant with varieties available in pink, yellow, and white. During June through September, long spikes of flowers appear.

Death Camas:

Edible camas and deadly camas look similar. However, they prefer drier soil conditions, often on hillsides or sagebrush slopes, especially in alpine forests. They occur in similar settings. Humans, animals, and even insects are poisoned by this plant's various sections (except for a particular species of mining bee, which has adapted to tolerate its toxins). Root bulbs, mature leaves, and seeds contain the most intense alkaloid toxicity concentrations. This plant can kill you if you eat just 2% to 6% of your body weight. Excessive salivation, tremors, weakness, loss of control over body movement, convulsions, coma, and death are all possible outcomes.

These toxic look-alikes can be easily distinguished from the edible camas by their blooming from April to July. Death camas blooms are greenish-white or cream in colour and smaller in size than edible camas blossoms, which range in colour from deep blue or purple to pale lavender. The solitary, unbranched stems of death camas end in a cluster of white-green flower buds, the leaves of which resemble grass and are V-shaped. Unlike edible camas, these camas lack the onion door and are bitter to taste (but it's recommended not to eat them).

Poison hemlock (Conium maculatum):

Poison hemlock often confused these plants with other Apiaceae species, such as cow parsley, because of its resemblance to them. It has hollow, purple-blotched stems that can grow up to 2 meters tall. When fully grown, the plants emit an acrid odour that some have compared to that of urine from raccoons. It can grow in ditches, streams, and roadside verges, all of which have a high moisture content.

Pokeweed:

Native to the eastern US, the Midwest, and the South, as well as scattered growth in the far west of the country, this plant, also known as common pokeweed, dragon berry, or Virginia poke or poke sallet (salad), is widely cultivated.

Late summer and early fall are prime times for the pokeweed plant's (Phytolacca americana) blueberry-like fruits to ripen. Please beware of the blueberry-like appearance of these berries; they are extremely poisonous. Roots, leaves, and stems are tainted with the highest poisons, followed by ripe fruit. In addition, the berries are poisonous when they are still green.

Chemicals throughout the plant cause vomiting, spasms, convulsions, bloody diarrhoea, and respiratory paralysis if swallowed. Two hours after ingesting plant parts, nausea and vomiting normally begin. Pokeweed's sap and berry juice can be absorbed through the skin, so avoid touching any portions of the plant that aren't covered in clothing.

Despite the similarity between pokeweed berries and blueberries, the fruit cluster stalks (peduncles) distinguish them. The stalks of pokeweed berry are a vibrant purplish pink, whereas the stalks of blueberry are a greenish-blue.

Its medium-green, silky leaves measure around 16 inches long. It's not just their appearance that makes them unappealing. Blueberry leaves, on the other hand, are oval, dark green, and up to two inches long.

Dogbane:

Dogbane, or Indian hemp, can be difficult to tell apart from milkweed because of its resemblance to both. Both plants are native to the same regions of the United States, and when the stems or leaves are broken, they both exude a white latex.

Examine the stem and leaves closely to tell the two plants apart. In contrast to dogbane, the stems of dogbane are reddish-coloured and tougher in texture. Milkweed's hairy leaves have a thicker, sturdier texture than this plant's leaves. The blooms are another aesthetic difference. Unlike dogbane, milkweed's blossoms range from light pink to purple and are rarely all-white, whereas dogbanes are white or greenish-white.

You can try a small amount of latex on your finger to see whether it's to your liking. The taste will be quite bitter if it is dogbane. Rinse your mouth and spit it out as soon as possible. If the flavour is a little sweet, you've identified the edible common milkweed plant and can proceed to pick the plant's stems, leaves, and flower or seed pods.

Apocynum means "poisonous to dogs" in the plant's botanical name. Eating any component of this plant can result in cardiac arrest and death in humans. Dogbane has been frequently employed by Native American tribes for its medicinal benefits despite the plant's toxicity. Whooping cough, asthma, rheumatism, pox, internal parasites, and diarrhoea are among medical conditions that can be treated. Venereal warts were treated externally with milky sap. The dried root of the plant was used to cure heart illness and expel parasitic worms by making a weak tea.

Certain modern-day herbal healers still use dogbane as a natural cure for many disorders. Even when taken orally, it must be done so under the direction of a licenced medical professional.

Cultivate Your Wide Plant

Home gardening has long been a gratifying pastime, and it's one of the best ways to ensure your family is eating the best possible produce. Household gardens are often handed down from generation to generation.

When caring for plants, many home farmers have likely been exposed to this lifestyle early and have an instinctual talent for knowing what a plant requires and when it requires it. Even if you've never done home gardening, you may still learn the skills necessary to be just as proficient as someone who has.

Most individuals who want to start producing fruits and vegetables at home often put it off because they fear it would be too expensive or need too much skill. In actuality, it is a straightforward process. The initial learning curve is, of course, steep. You may lose some plants, or the seeds may not germinate. If they do, you may not obtain any fruit at all at the beginning. Plants will respond to your soil type and the environment if you try to learn what works best for them.

To properly cultivate fruits and vegetables at home, you must go through several steps. The ability to maintain the plant life as long as possible, especially if you are cultivating plants that provide fruit frequently, comes first, followed by the actual development of the fruits. There are hurdles in every step of the process, but once you get it right, it's a truly fulfilling experience

There has been an increase in the cost of vegetables and fruits in recent years, and organic ones are much more costly. You can make even higher-quality things at home, saving money and giving yourself a sense of accomplishment. Additionally, cultivating an edible garden in your yard is a wonderful way to get your children interested in growing their food and getting them outside to enjoy the fresh air and sunshine.

Selecting the Site

There are a variety of ways to grow plants outside. Plants can be grown in smaller pots or long patio containers if you do not have a backyard. Vertical potting systems allow you to grow plants even if you don't have a lot of room on your patio. The best way to start a kitchen garden is with a small land area and expand as you gain experience and confidence.

Even if you have a vast property area, maintaining all those plants can be a lot of effort. To better understand how your planets interact with your environment, start with a tiny batch of plants. Then, you may plan your next batch of cultivation accordingly. Be aware that it will appear vacant for a while before the plants start to develop if your outside space is highly visible or positioned where you see it straight away as you enter your house. It will take at least a few months to cover an area with even the fastest-growing veggies. To avoid the space looking bare, either leave enough plants there to cover it or find another site.

Additionally, if you'll be using this spot regularly, and it's located in an area with many ornamental plants, the problem of not damaging your crops must be considered. If bugs or parasites infest your edible plants, your ornamental plants could also be infested, so be careful when walking through them.

If you'd like the best of both worlds, consider designing an ornamental landscape. With this method, you may use both edible and decorative plants in the same place to create an aesthetically appealing environment. Flowering food plants provide a lovely addition to a flowerbed because they complement the other more beautiful blooms.

It's important to ensure that your growing area gets enough sunlight, whether your plants are in pots or on the ground. As the seasons change, it can be difficult to know where your plants will get the most sunlight if they grow in the ground, especially if you are planting in the spring or fall, when sunlight exposure can vary greatly. You can always add some shade if there is too much light, but if there is not enough light, it can be difficult to overcome this problem in an outdoor situation.

Growing Guidelines

You can learn a lot about your area and environment by looking at the 'tech specs' of the plants you intend to cultivate and the seeds you have. It is important to note that the hardiness of seeds and plants might vary. Cold climates can be ideal for some, while others like the heat. As a general rule, some plants require more watering than others. Other factors to consider are how much sunshine each plant needs for optimal growth; some plants can't survive if exposed to direct sunlight for an extended period of time. When it comes to growing your food, there are many factors to consider.

The amount of time it takes to develop a certain vegetable or fruit is also important. For example, cilantro, mint, and coriander can be harvested within a few weeks, yet walnut and apple trees can take years to produce their first fruit.

An apple tree needs at least an 8-foot diameter to mature properly, but a 6-inch container will easily provide enough fruit to last many weeks. People misjudge the size of the plants and their needs. They risk cramming an area with too many plants. All of the plants are unable to grow correctly when this occurs. Only a dozen seeds will grow; even then, none will be large enough to bear fruit. This is a waste of time and money for farmers.

Distinct plants have different requirements for their growth. For example, if you want to grow vine-like veggies like cucumbers or squash, you'll want to set up a vine network that the vines may follow.

Ideally, you should have some elevated platform or frame where the plant grows. Keeping the soil dry will help keep the crops from rotting. Having some sticks in the ground to attach the plant to will help it grow taller, develop more leaves and stems, and produce more tomatoes in other circumstances, such as with tomato plants.

What is widely cultivated in your area will help you figure out what will work best in your area. You may learn a lot from the plants already flourishing in your region, even if local farmers raise them for profit. There will be more delicate types, of course, but this will give you a decent idea of what may be grown easily in the natural environment. There are several great resources on the USDA website, including information on cultivating specific fruits and vegetables that are appropriate for your region.

Growing something that requires a different set of conditions in an artificial environment, such as a greenhouse, is a viable choice if you have the resources to do so. People who cultivate their food do so partly because they can grow things that aren't readily available in their local area.

Farming Your Plants

People who have been farming for a long time may not understand that there are many more edible plants than the fruits and vegetables we see in shops. In your area, you're likely to find a wide variety of plants that are both edible and produce edible by-products.

Soil

Get a soil test done to understand what you're dealing with. Many garden soils are dry due to decades, if not centuries, of grass, decorative plants, weeds, and shrubs growing on them. All kinds of weather conditions stomped on, and no solid nutrients have ever been put to it. Furthermore, the soil texture is often too oily, clay-like, or sandy to grow anything, making it difficult. This method works well for fruit-bearing plants and vegetables, but it's a poor choice for grass and weeds.

You must conduct a soil test to get off to the greatest possible start. Crop farming is hard on the soil, especially with a tiny plot. As a result, you'll need to replenish the soil with additives from time to time.

Maintaining the soil

Organic food is grown in a way that is distinct from conventionally grown food. It is important to know what kind of fertilizer, pesticide, and chemical has been applied to alter or speed up the growth of the soil. If the original seed was genetically modified, then this is another factor.

All soil care solutions aim to alter the pH of the soil. A pH of roughly 6-7 is ideal, which means it's somewhat neutral. In addition, the nutrients needed by the plants should be included in a proportionate amount. An overabundance of nutrients in the soil can "burn" the plant, while a deficiency results in undernourished plants.

Fertilizers and Compost

If you want to speed up the process and lower the quality of your output, you don't need commercial-grade fertilizers. The best way to get the soil in the right condition is to utilize only organic soil additives. As a further step, establish a compost or mulch area in your garden and decompose your waste. All kinds of organic kitchen waste can be added to the mulch patch, including bread, vegetable tips, skins, and even eggshells. Organic compost will organically degrade all of this over time. Using soil additives is okay until you build your mulch, but once you do, you'll want to switch to utilizing it exclusively.

Various organic pest control sprays, pellets, and soil amendments are available. When you're just starting, this won't be a big worry, but as the garden gets thicker, especially when vegetables and fruits begin to grow, you'll have to deal with more pests. Another reason to keep your plants well-spaced is to ensure that the plants and the soil have access to enough air circulation. Soil chokes and tightens in a highly populated kitchen garden because of a lack of oxygen. You should be able to get into the soil from time to time to till it and replenish it with fresh soil from deeper in the ground. As a result, the plants will receive more oxygenation from the ground up.

Make certain that the ground is as level as possible as well. Depending on the shape, water pools or run-off without soaking into the soil for concave or convex. It may not be a problem at first, but as the crop grows and water management becomes more difficult, it will become a problem that will deteriorate the soil's quality.

Water

The quality of the ground or surface water you're drawing from should be examined before you use it, especially if the water comes from a deep underground well or a nearby lake. Just make sure the water isn't too "hard," meaning it doesn't contain excessive amounts of minerals and is also free of contamination. As long as the water is acceptable for human consumption, it should also be fine for the plants. Even if the water in your city isn't fit for human consumption, it might be beneficial to plants if the concentration of minerals isn't excessive.

Edible Wild Plant Recipes

1. Burdock Mushroom Rice

Ingredients:

- 4 large mushrooms
- 1 medium Burdock root
- Salted water for soaking Burdock root
- 1 cup brown rice
- 3 tablespoons miso
- 3 tablespoons butter
- 1 grated carrot

Directions:

1. Soak Burdock roots in salted water for 5 minutes, then drain.
2. Add miso and 2 cups water to a cooking pot, then cook to a boil.
3. Stir in rice and cook until the rice is soft. Sauté Burdock roots with butter in a skillet for 5 minutes.
4. Stir in mushrooms and carrots, then cook for 5 minutes.
5. Serve warm with the miso rice.

2. Milkweed Rice

Ingredients:

- 1 cup basmati rice
- 1 cup vegetable stock
- 1/2 cup Milkweed flower buds

- 1/2 cup white wine

- 3 garlic cloves, chopped

- 3 tablespoons yellow onions, chopped

- 3 tablespoons butter

- 1 tablespoon olive oil

- Parmesan cheese, grated

- Sea salt and/or pepper, to taste

Direction:

1. Add stock, wine, and rice to a cooking pot, then cook to a boil.
2. Reduce the heat and cook on a simmer until liquid is absorbed.
3. Sauté onions and garlic with butter and oil in a skillet for 5 minutes.
4. Stir in Milkweed flower buds and cook for 1 minute.
5. Add rice and mix well. Serve warm.

3. Cattail Rice

Ingredients:

- 1 tsp Pepper

- 2 c Vegetable broth,

- 5 tsp Garlic salt

- 1 c Uncooked rice

- Diced onion

- 1 c Chopped young cattail shoots

- 2 tbsp + 1 tbsp Butter

Direction:

1. Start by adding the two tablespoons of butter to a pan and letting it melt. Add in the cattail shoots and cook until they are soft. This will take about five to ten minutes. If you need to, you can add in the extra better. Once soft, turn the heat down to low and add in the onions, pepper, and garlic, cooking until translucent.

2. As your veggies are cooking, cook your rice according to the package directions. If you need to, adjust the rice to water ratio according to the directions.

3. After the rice has been cooked, mix in the cooked vegetables. Cover the pot and let everything sit for two to three minutes. Enjoy.

4. Mediterranean Dock Soup with Lemon and Rice

Ingredients:

- 6 ounces Fresh and soft curly dock leaves
- Kosher salt - to taste
- Fresh lemon juice - to taste
- 2 tbsp Extra virgin olive oil - (you will need more for drizzling)
- 4 cups   Vegetable or chicken stock
- ¼ cups Basmati rice
- 1 small yellow onion
- 1 tbsp Chopped garlic
- 1 egg (beaten)
- Optional: fresh oregano or monarda fistulosa - to taste (chopped)
- A hint of ground cumin
- Water

Directions:

1. Salt some water and boil it to blanch the curly dock inside. Leave it until it wilts, which should take no longer than a few seconds. Transfer the dock into cold water to cool. Take it out and squeeze out as much water as you can.

2. Heat the oven to 176.6 degrees Celsius or 350 degrees Fahrenheit and leave it until it's golden. Take it out and set it aside to cool.

3. Add the rice, ½ a cup of water, and a hint of salt into a put. Turn on the heat and bring it to a simmer. Cover the pot and allow the rice to cook until it's tender.

4. Chop coarse dock leaves (you can cut them in a cross-hatch-like pattern to ensure that there aren't any long pieces).

5. Dice the garlic and onion and place them on medium-high heat for 10 minutes. The edges should be somewhat brown by then.

6. Add the dock leaves, stock, oregano, and a hint of cumin. Bring to a simmer and season with pepper and salt to taste. Add the rice and simmer it on low heat for 10 more minutes.

7. Stir in the egg and allow it to heat. Drizzle with olive oil, black pepper, and a lot of fresh lemon juice to serve.

5. Pilau Rice with Wild Garlic and Stinging Nettles

Ingredients

- 500 ml stock
- 1 ¼ cups rice
- ⅔ cups black lentils
- 2 onions
- 2 carrots
- ¾ cups wild garlic
- 1 cup nettles
- pinch of crushed red chili

- ⅓ cup black olives
- ½ tsp black pepper
- 1 tsp pink Himalayan salt
- 1 tbsp fried onions
- 2 tbsp pine nuts
- 2 tbsp olive oil

Direction:

1. Over medium heat, heat up the oil in a pan, add the onions, sliced carrots, finely chopped garlic, pinch of salt, and black pepper. Cook for 2-3 minutes.
2. Pour in the stock and bring to a boil.
3. Bring to simmer, then add rice and black lentils and let it cook on low heat for 7-8 minutes. The pan should be covered.
4. Take the lid off, add the nettles and wild garlic. Season, if necessary.
5. Mix well, add in the olives and cook for another 5 minutes on low. Once done, sprinkle chili flakes and pine nuts on top.

6. Burdock Shitake Rice

Ingredients:

- 3 cups cooked rice
- 3 tablespoons coconut oil
- 1 large onion, diced
- 3 garlic cloves, minced

- 1/2 teaspoon fresh ginger, minced
- 1 medium carrot, diced
- 1/4 cup peas
- 5 shitake mushrooms, diced
- 1 Burdock Root, diced
- 2 eggs
- 3 tablespoons soy sauce
- 1 green onion, chopped

Direction:

1. Soak Burdock in a bowl with water for 20 minutes, then drain.
2. Toss the Burdock with 1 tablespoon coconut oil in a bowl, then keep it aside.
3. Beat eggs in a bowl and keep them aside.
4. Sauté onion with 2 tablespoons coconut oil in a wok for 5 minutes. Stir carrots, ginger, and garlic, then cook until soft.
5. Add peas, mushroom, and burdock root, then cook for 1 minute. Push the vegetables aside and pour in the eggs.
6. Scramble and cook the eggs, then add soy sauce and rice. Mix well, then garnish with green onion. Serve warm.

7. Fennel Greens Rice

Ingredients:

- 1/4 cup unsalted butter
- 2 dozen wild onions, chopped
- 1 garlic clove, minced
- 1 1/2 cups arborio rice
- Salt, to taste

- 1 cup white wine
- 1 cup chicken broth
- 1/4 cup chopped Fennel greens
- 3 tablespoons minced Fennel fronds
- 1/3 cup grated Parmigiano cheese

Direction:

1. Sauté onion with 3 tablespoons butter in a suitable cooking pot for 6 minutes.
2. Stir in garlic and cook for 1 minute.
3. Add rice and cook for 5 minutes. Stir in white wine, salt, chicken broth and cook on a simmer until the liquid is absorbed.
4. Add chopped Fennel greens, grated cheese, and Fennel fronds.
5. Garnish with butter and serve warm.

8. Plantain Salad

Ingredients:

- 2 cups of wild plantain leaves, finely chopped
- 1 can of chickpeas, well-drained
- ½ cup of finely chopped cabbage
- 1 finely chopped celery stalk
- 1 finely chopped garlic clove
- 1/8 cup of olive oil
- 1/8 cup of vinegar
- 1 tsp salt

Direction:

1. Mix all the ingredients (exclude oil and vinegar) in a big bowl and put them in the refrigerator.
2. Allow to chill, then add the vinegar and oil.

3. If the salad is too dry for you, add more oil and vinegar equally until you achieve the right moistness for your taste buds.

9. Speedwell Salad

Ingredients:

- Fresh Speedwell leaves
- Other fruits of your choosing
- Sour cream

Direction:

1. Chop the speedwell leaves and the fruits.
2. Transfer to a bowl and spread the sour cream on it.
3. Serve and enjoy.

10. Purslane Salad

Ingredients:

- 1/4 cup red onion, sliced
- 1 lemon, zested and juiced
- 1 tablespoon red wine vinegar
- 1 bunch Purslane, chopped
- 2 tablespoons olive oil
- 2 tablespoons plain yogurt

- Pinch salt
- Pinch black pepper
- 1/2 cup feta cheese
- 1/2 cucumber, chopped
- 3/4 cup melon, cubed
- 5 radishes, sliced

Direction:

1. Toss onion with Purslane and the rest of the ingredients in a salad bowl.
2. Serve.

11. Seaweed Salad

Ingredients:

- 1 package of seaweed
- 4 scallions, chopped
- 1/3 cup seasoned rice vinegar
- 2 tablespoons sesame oil
- 3 cloves garlic, minced

Directions:

1. Rinse the seaweed under water to remove any excess salt. Chop the seaweed into small, bite-sized pieces.
2. Mix the vinegar, sesame oil, garlic, and scallions in a large bowl. Add in seaweed and let it marinate for at least 30 minutes. Serve chilled or at room temperature.

12. Burdock Tuna Salad

Ingredients:

- 1 can of tuna (drain and break apart)
- 2 burdock roots, peeled
- 2 tbsp ground sesame seed (white)
- 3 tbsp mayonnaise
- 1 tsp vinegar
- 1 tsp soy sauce
- 1 tsp sugar

Direction:

1. Mix all the ingredients (except tuna and burdock roots) in a large bowl and place them aside.
2. Put the peeled burdock roots into your saucepan and pour in enough water to cover. Let it boil for 5 minutes. Then, drain and leave the burdock to cool.
3. Add the burdock and tuna to the ingredients in the large bowl and mix in well. Cover and leave it in the fridge for 30 minutes.
4. Before serving, stir the meal one more time. Note that you can add cheese or grated carrot to the meal if you like. The meal shouldn't take more than 2o minutes for both prepping and cooking, and it should serve up to 4 people.

13. Mustard and Wood Sorrel Salad

Ingredients:

- 1 tablespoon white wine vinegar
- ½ teaspoon salt

- A few grinds of black pepper
- 3 tablespoons sunflower oil
- ½ cup wood sorrel leaves, chopped
- 1 teaspoon crushed mustard seed
- 1 tablespoon bacon bits (optional)

Directions:

1. Whisk the vinegar, salt, and pepper in a small bowl. Slowly add sunflower oil while whisking.
2. Combine the wood sorrel, mustard seed, bacon bits (optional), and dressing in a large bowl and toss until coated well. Serve immediately.

14. Chickweed Salad

Ingredients:

- 3 cups Chickweed, (chopped)
- ¼ cup purple daikon radish (cut into small sticks)
- ¼ cup Carrots (cut into small sticks)
- 1 ½ tbsp Extra virgin olive oil
- 1 tbsp Kombucha vinegar
- 1 tbsp Fresh lemon juice
- Hawaiian red sea salt to taste (can be substituted for pink sea salt)

Directions:

1. Chop up your vegetables. The radish and the carrots must be cut into small sticks because otherwise, they may overwhelm the salad. Chickweed is a very fine green.
2. Combine the extra virgin olive oil, the kombucha vinegar (or other salad vinegar), and the fresh lemon or blood orange juice in a bowl. Whisk well.

3. Pour the liquid onto the vegetables and toss well.

4. Sprinkle the Hawaiian red or pink sea salt onto the salad and toss once more. Make sure that the amount of salad is ideal for your taste.

5. Plate your salad and sprinkle some lemon zest on it.

15. Dandelion Green and Potato Salad

Ingredients

- 2 cups of potatoes
- large bunch of dandelion greens
- 3 tbsp olive oil
- 2 garlic cloves
- 1 head of chicory
- 1 can white kidney beans
- zest and juice of a lemon
- 2 tbsp ricotta
- salt and pepper

Direction:

1. Boil the potatoes, drain and slice in half. While the potatoes are boiling, trim the dandelions and chicory. Rinse and cut into large pieces.

2. Heat up the olive oil, add the garlic and stir until it turns golden.

3. Add the greens and sauté for around 2-3 minutes. Season with salt and pepper.

4. Add the kidney beans and the potatoes to the pan. Mix everything together and add the zest, lemon juice, and ricotta.

5. Toss everything, so everything is evenly coated. Check the seasoning and add salt and pepper if necessary.

16. Claytonia and Arugula Salad (Claytonia)

Ingredients:

- 1 c. claytonia leaves
- Salt and pepper to taste
- 2 tbsp. vinegar
- 6 tbsp. olive oil
- ½ c. toasted nuts
- 1 c. green apple
- 2 c. chopped arugula

Direction:

1. Add the greens into a single bowl.
2. Add the nuts and apples to the greens in the bowl.
3. Add pepper, salt, vinegar, and oil to another container and mix.
4. Drizzle the sauce over the salad and serve.

17. Henbit Salad

Ingredients:

- 4 c. Henbit shoots
- 3 tbsp. butter
- 1 tsp. curry powder
- 2 whole cloves
- ¼ tsp. ground cinnamon
- 2 tbsp. flour
- 3 c. sour cream

Direction:

1. Chop four cups of henbit. Pour into a pot and cover with water.

2. Place on a stove and let it boil for about 10 minutes.

3. Add the butter to another pan and add the ground cinnamon, cloves, and curry powder. Stir and allow to cook for 1 minute.

4. Add boiling water to the henbit and continue stirring until it becomes smooth.

5. Drain and pour the boiled henbit together with 3 cups of sour cream.

6. Let it cook for another 15 minutes and serve.

18. Shepherd's Purse Soup

Ingredients:

- 8 oz. frozen shepherd purse
- 3 eggs whites
- ¼ corn-starch
- ¼ tsp. ground white pepper
- 1 tsp. sesame oil
- 1 ½ tsp. salt
- 4 c. homemade chicken stock
- ½ block of silken tofu

Direction:

1. Thaw the shepherd's purse. After, squeeze out the water in it and chop the leaves. Cut the tofu into half cubes.

2. Heat the chicken stock in a medium pot, then add salt, ground white pepper, and sesame oil.

3. Add corn-starch and water, and then mix. Reduce the heat and drizzle the corn-starch slurry slowly into the soup. Continue stirring.

4. Turn on the heat as you stir. Add salt to taste too. Allow the soup to simmer for a minute.

5. Add the tofu cubes and stir. Allow the soup to simmer for about 4 minutes and add corn-starch slurry if you want the soup to be thicker.

19. Buttered Chickweed

Ingredients:

- 2 cups of chopped chickweed
- 1 finely chopped green onion
- Butter
- Salt
- Pepper

Directions:

1. Clean the chickweed thoroughly in cold water. Then, pour into boiling salted water. Let it cook for three minutes before you drain the water. You can keep the liquid to make tea or rice later.
2. Melt a tiny amount of butter in your stir-fry pan. Pour in the onions and sauté until it is soft and translucent. Then, pour in the chickweed. Add salt, pepper, and other spices that you like. Continue to sauté for 1 to 2 minutes.
3. Serve for two people.

20. Wild Plant Quesadilla

Ingredients:

- 4 tortillas
- 12 ramps, chopped (wild leeks)
- 1 tablespoon garlic salt
- Olive oil

- 2 cups Mexican cheese blend, shredded

Directions:

1. Brush the bottom of a large pan with olive oil and heat over medium heat.

2. Fry the ramps for 4-5 minutes until they soften. Add garlic salt and stir well.

3. Cover half of one side of each tortilla with cheese, then top with ramps and fold the tortillas in half.

4. Cook on each side until golden brown, around 4 minutes per side.

5. Remove from the pan and cut into wedges. Serve immediately.

21. Wild Roasted Cabbage

Ingredients:

- 5 slices Crumbled cooked bacon, if desired

- Grated cheese if desired

- Pepper and salt

- Ground dried stinging nettle, to taste

- Chopped garlic, to taste

- Chopped onion, to taste

- Chopped garlic mustard, to taste

- 4 to 6 tbsp Olive oil

- Head of cabbage

Direction:

1. Start by getting your oven to 350.

2. Lay the cabbage on a chopping board and slice into ¼ inch thick slices. Do your best to hold the leaves together. You can usually get four to six slices.

3. Brush the bottom of the slices with oil and then lay them on a parchment-lined baking sheet.

4. Add the rest of the oil to a bowl and combine with the garlic, pepper, salt, and nettle. Brush this on top of the cabbage slices.

5. Sprinkle the tops of the cabbage with the onions and garlic mustard.

6. Bake this for 20 minutes. Take out and top with the cheese and bacon if you are using them. Let this back for about 15 minutes more. Enjoy.

22. Oven-Baked Acorn Squash

Ingredients:

- 1 acorn squash, cut in half and seeds removed
- Butter or vegan margarine to taste

Directions:

1. Preheat oven to 400°F.
2. Place the acorn squash, cut side up, on a baking sheet.
3. Rub the flesh with butter or vegan margarine to taste.
4. Bake for 45-50 minutes, until soft. Serve immediately.

23. Dandelion Pumpkin Seed Pesto

Ingredients

- ¾ cup pumpkin seeds
- ¼ cup grated parmesan
- 3 garlic cloves
- 2 cups dandelion greens
- ½ cup olive oil
- 1 tbsp. lemon juice
- ½ teaspoon salt

- black pepper

Direction:

1. Preheat the oven to 350°F. Roast the pumpkin seeds until fragrant, roughly 5 minutes. Once done, take out of the oven and cool.
2. Add the garlic and pumpkin seeds to a food processor and chop into fine pieces.
3. Add the cheese, dandelions, and lemon juice and process until everything is combined. You may need to stop occasionally to scrape down the sides. It might be quite thick and hard to process, so give it a while.
4. Add the oil and process until the pesto is a smooth paste. Add your salt and pepper.

Buttered Chickweed

You'll Need:

Pepper

Salt

Butter

Finely chopped onion

Chopped chickweed, 2 c

You'll Do:

Start by washing the chickweed. Bring a pot of salted water to a boil and add the chickweed into the water. Let this cook for a couple of minutes and then drain well.

Add some butter to a pan. Add in the onion and sauté until translucent. Add in the chickweed. Season with some pepper and salt or any other spices that you would like.

24. Plantain Salad

Ingredients:

- 1 tsp Salt
- 1/8 c Wine vinegar
- 1/8 c Olive oil
- 1 to 2 cloves Chopped garlic
- Finely chopped celery stalk
- Thinly chopped onion
- A Can of drained chickpeas
- 5 c Finely chopped cabbage
- 2 c Chopped plantain

Direction:

1. Start by mixing all of the above ingredients together, except for the vinegar and oil. Place the in the refrigerator. Once this has chilled well, add in the vinegar and oil.
2. If you find that the salad is a bit on the dry side, you can add some more vinegar and olive oil. Taste and adjust any seasonings that you need to.

25. Wild Potato Pancakes

Ingredients:

- 1 tsp Pepper
- 1 tsp Salt
- 2 tsp Garlic powder

- 2 tbsp Flour
- 2 tbsp Hemp seeds
- 25 c Chopped mushrooms
- 5 c Chopped wild greens
- 33 c Chopped onions
- 2Eggs
- 4 c Grated potatoes

Direction:

1. Start by melting some butter in a pan. Add the onions and sauté for a couple of minutes and then mix in the mushrooms. Cook for another two minutes and set it off of the heat.

2. In a bowl, add the spices, flour, seeds, eggs, sautéed vegetables, and grated potatoes. Mix everything together for about three minutes to make sure everything is well combined.

3. In a frying pan, melt a bit of butter to make sure the pancakes don't stick. With your hands, create balls from the batter. As you do this, you will notice that the potatoes contain some liquid. Squeeze out some of this liquid.

4. Lay the ball onto the frying pan and flatten it with a spatula to about a half-inch thick. Cook until both sides are golden brown. Add extra butter if you need to so that they don't stick.

5. Continue until all of the batter is used and enjoy.

26. Creamy Potato and Wild Garlic Mash

Ingredients

- 4 ½ cups floury potatoes
- ½ cup unsalted butter
- ½ cup per wild garlic leaves
- double cream

- nutmeg

Direction:

1. Place potatoes in a pan with cold saltwater and boil. Once it has come to a boil, simmer for 20 minutes until tender.
2. Drain the water and add the potatoes back to the pan to dry out on low heat. Don't keep them on heat for too long.
3. Melt the butter in another pan and fry the wild garlic for 30 seconds.
4. Mash the potatoes, add a generous dash of cream, nutmeg, and garlic butter.
5. Taste, adjust seasoning and serve.

27. Garlic Mustard Pesto

Ingredients:

- 11 c. packed garlic mustard leaves
- 2 squeezes of lemon juice
- ½ tsp. sugar
- ½ tsp. salt
- 12 c. extra virgin olive oil
- ⅓ c. grated parmesan cheese
- 1 garlic clove
- ¼ c. pine nuts

Direction:

1. Pour the parmesan, pine nuts, and garlic into a blender and blend. Add the garlic mustard.
2. Pour the olive oil steadily for about 1 minute into the blender and continue blending until the mixture is smooth.
3. Add lemon juice, sugar, pulse, and salt until they are well mixed.
4. Serve and enjoy.

28. Himalayan Balsam Curry

Ingredients:

- Himalayan balsam seed
- 1 onion
- Olive oil
- 1 swede
- 2 tbsp. Curry paste
- 2 sticks of celery
- 2 tomatoes
- 2 red peppers

Direction:

1. Slice the onion and pour it into a pan. Pour the olive oil into a pan.

2. Add the sliced onion and fry gently until it becomes translucent. Cut the swede into small cubes and pour into a bowl.

3. Add the curry paste to the mixture on the stove and mix. Allow everything to fry for 1 minute. After 1 minute, add the Himalayan balsam and stir.

4. Add the swede to the mixture on the stove. Add hot water to cover the saucepan. Add the sticks of celery and creamed coconut.

5. Chop the tomatoes and add to the pan. Slice the red pepper thinly and also add. Allow simmering until the vegetables become tender. Serve and enjoy.

29. Andalusian Mallow with Chickpea (Mallow Species)

Ingredients:

- 4 tsp. cumin seeds
- A bagful of mallow leaves
- ½ bulb of crushed garlic
- A large jar of drained chickpeas
- Juice of a lemon
- Salt to taste
- Olive oil

Direction:

1. Rinse the mallow leaves and slice roughly.
2. Add leaves to a pan containing water and steam on low heat.
3. Pour the cumin seeds into a large frying pan and dry toast it. Grind in a grinder.
4. Fry the cumin using olive oil on medium heat, add the garlic, and stir.
5. Add the chickpea and stir in the mellow. Let it cook for about 15 minutes and add water if it dries up. Add lemon juice and salt to taste, and then serve.

30. Lotus Root Stir Fry

Ingredients:

- 1 lb. fresh Lotus Root, peeled
- 1 tablespoon ginger, sliced
- 1 tablespoon garlic, sliced

- 3 tablespoons sesame oil
- 3 tablespoons vegetable stock
- 1 tablespoon soy sauce
- 3 teaspoons rice wine vinegar
- 1/2 teaspoon salt
- 1/4 cup peanuts
- red chilli pepper flakes, to taste
- 3 green onions, chopped

Direction:

1. Mix 1 tablespoon sesame oil, soy sauce, stock, and vinegar in a small bowl.
2. Sauté peanuts with 2 tablespoons oil in a skillet until golden brown.
3. Remove these peanuts from the heat and set them aside.
4. Sauté Lotus Root with ginger, garlic and vinegar mixture for 5 minutes.
5. Stir in the rest of the ingredients, then cook for 5 minutes. Serve warm.

31. Wild Curly Dock Masala (Curly Dock)

Ingredients:

- ½ c. onion
- ¼ c. fresh coriander leaves
- ½ tbsp. pan-toasted mustard seeds
- 4 c. curly dock leaves, de-stemmed and washed
- 2 tsp. Freshly grated ginger
- ½ tsp. salt to taste
- 4 tsp. homemade gram masala
- 2 c. coconut milk

Direction:

1. Pour all the ingredients into a dry pan before grinding the mustard seeds. Add the masala and mix until evenly combined. Add salt to taste

2. Add the curly dock, coating it with the aromatics and spice mixture.

3. Cool and blend until it appears smooth. It is now ready for serving.

32. Sauteed Watercress with Garlic

Ingredients:

- 2 tbsp. olive oil
- 2 bunches of rinsed and trimmed watercress
- 6 minced and grated garlic cloves

Direction:

1. Pour the oil into a skillet and put it on medium heat. Add the garlic and sauté until it gives out a fragrance.

2. Add the watercress and salt. Allow to cook and stir while cooking for about 40 seconds.

3. Add two tablespoons of water and stir again until the leaves wilt.

33. Irish Colcannon with Wild Greens

Ingredients:

- 2 lbs. potatoes, peeled and diced
- Salt, to taste

- 3 cups of Wild Greens, chopped
- 1 cup chopped green onions
- 1 cup half-and-half milk
- 5 tablespoons butter

Direction:

1. Add water, a pinch of salt and potatoes to a cooking pot. Cook for 20 minutes, then drain.
2. Sauté greens and onions with 2 tablespoons butter in a skillet.
3. Stir in Wild Greens and cook for 3 minutes.
4. Add half and half, butter, and drained potatoes.
5. Lightly mash the potatoes and serve warm.

34. Butternut Squash Soup

Ingredients:

- 2 to 3 pounds of butternut squash
- Nutmeg
- 6 c. chicken stock
- 1 medium chopped onion
- 2 tbsp. unsalted butter

Direction:

1. Cut the squash into chunks.
2. Melt butter in a large pot. Add the onions and cook for about 8 hours.
3. Add squash and stock. Simmer and cook for 20 minutes until tender. Remove squash chunks using a slotted spoon.
4. Place in a blender and puree.
5. Return the blended squash to the pot. Stir and add pepper, salt, and nutmeg to season

35. Cattail Soup

Ingredients:

- 1 cup of lower segments cattail shoots, young and tender
- 1 green onion
- 5 buttons of mushrooms
- ½ cup of parboiled rice
- 4 cups of vegetable stock
- 2 cloves of garlic
- 2 tsp of turmeric
- 1 tsp of black pepper
- Salt

Direction:

1. Chop the cattail shoots, garlic cloves, onions, and mushrooms into fine pieces.
2. Place a frying pan over medium-low heat and sauté the cattail in a fine amount of olive oil or butter. Do this for 10 minutes or until the shoots are tender.
3. Add a little more oil or butter if needed, then continue to sauté. Next, add the garlic, onions, and mushrooms. Continue until the onions become translucent.
4. Set the vegetable stock into a fairly-sized saucepan. Let it heat to boiling level, then turn down the heat. Add the sautéed greens and spices into the pan, and stir well. Allow simmering for 15 to 20 minutes before you add in the parboiled rice.
5. Let it cook for five more minutes, then serve. Don't forget to add salt and other seasonings to taste. Just make sure they don't ruin the meal's taste.

36. Stinging Nettle Soup

Ingredients:

- 1 tablespoon butter
- 3 onions, chopped
- 5 cloves garlic, minced
- 2 tablespoons fresh oregano, chopped
- 1 cup wild rice, cooked
- 1 teaspoon salt
- A few grinds of black pepper
- 6 cups chicken broth
- 1 cup milk
- ½ teaspoon nutmeg
- A few stalks of stinging nettle, chopped

Directions:

1. Melt the butter over medium heat in a large pan. Cook the onions for about 5 minutes until they soften.
2. Add the garlic and cook for another minute or two until you can smell it cooking. Stir in oregano.
3. Bring broth to a simmer in another pot. Add rice, milk, salt, and pepper to the onion mixture. Stir well and let simmer.
4. Once the broth is simmering, add chopped nettles and let cook for 5 minutes more. Stir occasionally to avoid burning.
5. Ladle the broth and nettles into bowls and serve immediately.

37. Sorrel Soup

Ingredients:

- 3 tablespoons unsalted butter
- 1/2 cup shallots, chopped
- 6 cups Wood Sorrel, chopped
- 1-litre vegetable stock
- 1/2 cup cream
- 1 pinch of salt

Direction:

1. Sauté onions with butter in a soup pot for 5 minutes. Stir in stock and cook to a simmer.
2. Add Sorrel leaves, salt, and cook for 10 minutes on a simmer with occasional stirring.
3. Add cream and cook for 5 minutes on a low heat. Serve warm.

38. Wood Sorrel Soup

Ingredients:

- 3 tbsps. of pure butter
- ½ cup of onions or shallots, finely chopped
- 4 cups of wood sorrel, finely chopped and packed
- 1 cup of cream
- 1 litre of vegetable stock
- Salt to taste

Direction:

1. Melt the unsalted butter in a medium-sized soup pot. Put in the chopped onions or shallots and turn on the heat, medium-low. Sauté for some minutes. Pour the vegetable stick and allow everything to simmer for 5 minutes.

2. Turn up the heat to medium, add the wood sorrel leaves, and put in a pinch of salt or adjust as needed, and stir together.

3. When the greens are wilted, reduce the heat once again. Cover the pot and allow the mixture to cook for 1o to 15 minutes. Stir occasionally until the soup is ready.

4. To finish, add the cream to the soup and let it simmer on low heat for at least 5 minutes. Serve immediately. Alternatively, you can refrigerate the soup and eat cold when you are ready. It tastes good both ways.

39. Fiddlehead Soup

Ingredients:

- 2 tablespoons butter
- 4 cloves garlic, chopped
- 1 onion, chopped
- 1 cup parsnips, chopped
- 3 cups potatoes, diced
- 6 cups chicken broth
- 2 teaspoons salt
- A few grinds of black pepper
- ½ cup green onions, chopped
- 2 cups fiddlehead ferns, chopped
- 1 tablespoon lemon juice

Directions:

1. Melt the butter in a large pot and add garlic and onion. Cook for 2 minutes, or until the garlic is fragrant and the onion is soft.

2. Add parsnips, potatoes, broth, salt, and pepper.

3. Bring to a boil over high heat, then simmer for 15-20 minutes or until the parsnips and potatoes are tender.

4. Add green onions, fiddleheads, and lemon juice. Cook for 5 more minutes until ferns are tender. Serve immediately.

---

40. Leek and Nettle Soup

Ingredients:

- 2 large potatoes
- 10 cups of water
- ½ cup of dried or fresh stinging nettle
- 4 cups of thinly sliced leeks (ramps)
- 1 handful of fresh dandelions, finely chopped
- 1 handful of fresh red clover, finely chopped
- 2 tsp of seasoning
- 1 tsp of pepper
- 1 tsp of salt
- 3 tsp of garlic powder
- 3 tsp of dulce flakes

Direction:

1. Parboil the potatoes in a large pot. Once tender, drain the water and rinse in a fresh pot.
2. Pour water into a large pot and add the stinging nettle. Boil on low heat and add the rest of the ingredients one by one, including the potatoes. Stir well and let it simmer for 30 minutes. F
3. ire up your blender and pour in the mixture. Turn for 10 to 30 seconds to make the soup more refined.
4. Pour the soup into serving bowls and garnish with an extra teaspoon of dulce flakes. If you have fresh parsley, you can add it to the soup to make it more garnished.

41. Nettle Soup

Ingredients

- ⅔ cup nettle tops
- ¼ cup butter
- 1 onion
- 1 leek, finely sliced
- 2 celery sticks, chopped
- 1 clove garlic, chopped
- 2 tbsp white rice
- 1-liter stock
- sea salt and ground pepper
- 6 tbsp plain yogurt
- dash of chives, to garnish

Direction:

1. Wash the nettles and get rid of the harder stalks. Melt butter in a pan on medium-low heat.
2. Add onion, leek, celery, garlic, and cover for 10 minutes. Stir if necessary and cook until everything is soft but not brown.
3. Add the rice and stock, bring it all to a simmer and cook for 10 minutes.
4. Add the nettles, and simmer for around 5 minutes. Both the nettles and rice should be succulent.
5. Season with salt and pepper. You can blend this until it is thin, reheat, if need be, and serve in bowls. You can add the yogurt and chives at this point for extra flavour.

42. Sorrel Soup

Ingredients

- 4 tbsp unsalted butter
- ½ cup chopped onion
- 4-6 cups chopped sorrel
- salt
- 1-quart stock (chicken or vegetable)
- 3 tbsp flour
- 2 egg yolks
- ½ cup cream

Direction:

1. In a large pot, melt the butter over medium heat. Add the onions, stir, and lower the heat to medium-low.
2. Cover the pot and cook for ten minutes.
3. Pour the stock into another pot and bring to a simmer. Increase the heat, add the sorrel leaves and a large pinch of salt to the onions. Once the sorrel is wilted, reduce the heat to medium-low, cover, and cook for 10 minutes.
4. Add the flour and cook on medium heat for 3 minutes. Whisk in the stock, ensure you keep stirring, and then bring to a simmer.
5. Whisk the egg yolk and cream nuts on top.

43. Chilled Lemony Wood Sorrel Soup

Ingredients:

- 2 cloves of minced garlic
- Olive oil
- 1 c. full-fat coconut milk

- 3 medium-sized mint leaves
- 2 c. lightly packed wood sorrel
- 2 c. of vegetable broth
- 2 chopped scallions
- Pepper and salt to taste

Direction:

1. Pour the olive oil into a small saucepan
2. Sauté the garlic until it starts producing fragrance, and then add scallions.
3. Cover the garlic with vegetable broth and boil.
4. Allow it to simmer for about 5 minutes, after which you can add sorrel for about 30 seconds
5. Remove from heat and add mint. Then blend smoothly
6. Add the coconut milk, salt, and pepper. Place in the refrigerator until chilled. Serve and enjoy.

44. Mug wort Soup

Ingredients:

- 3 tbsp. unsalted butter
- 1 medium onion
- 1 large Yukon gold
- 10 medium white mushrooms
- 2 cloves of minced garlic
- Coarse salt
- Tobacco
- 4 oz. tender mug wort
- 1 c. heavy cream

- 6 c. low-sodium chicken

Direction:

1. Add the butter to a pot and place it over medium heat to melt. Add the onion and allow it to sauté until it softens. Add the mushroom and garlic and cook until they soften.
2. Add potatoes and broth. Then allow boiling.
3. Lower heat and simmer for about 20 minutes.
4. Add the mug wort and cream and allow simmering for 10 minutes. Remove from heat and let cool.
5. Puree in batches using a blender and return to the pot.
6. Add adequate Tabasco to taste. Then add pepper and salt.

45. Shepherd's Purse Soup

Ingredients:

- 8 oz. frozen shepherd purse
- 3 eggs whites
- ¼ corn-starch
- ¼ tsp. ground white pepper
- 1 tsp. sesame oil
- 1 ½ tsp. salt
- 4 c. homemade chicken stock
- ½ block of silken tofu

Direction:

1. Thaw the shepherd's purse. After, squeeze out the water in it and chop the leaves. Cut the tofu into half cubes.
2. Heat the chicken stock in a medium pot, then add salt, ground white pepper, and sesame oil.

3. Add corn-starch and water, and then mix. Reduce the heat and drizzle the corn-starch slurry slowly into the soup. Continue stirring. Turn on the heat as you stir. Add salt to taste too.

4. Allow the soup to simmer for a minute.

5. Add the tofu cubes and stir. Allow the soup to simmer for about 4 minutes and add corn-starch slurry if you want the soup to be thicker.

46. Potato Wild Leek Soup

Ingredients:

- 3 large leeks
- 4 Wild Leeks
- 4 tablespoon Wild Leek powder
- 2 tablespoons butter
- 4 cups vegetable broth
- 2 lbs. potatoes, peeled, diced
- 1 teaspoon dried thyme
- 1/4 cup chopped fresh parsley
- Black pepper and garlic powder, to taste

Direction:

1. Sauté leeks with butter in a suitable cooking pot for 5 minutes.
2. Stir in potatoes and sauté for 5 minutes.
3. Add broth and the rest of the ingredients, then cook for 25 minutes.
4. Serve warm.

47. Blueberry Labrador Tea

Ingredients:

- 1 tbsp Lemon juice, if desired
- 1 c Water
- 1.5 c Blueberries
- 4 c Labrador tea

Direction:

1. Add the blueberries and water to a pot and let them come to a boil. Turn the heat down and simmer, stirring often, until the blueberries start to break down. This will take about five to ten minutes.
2. Add the blueberries into the brewed tea. Add in your favourite sweetener, stir, and then let it come to room temperature.
3. Place in the fridge until cold, usually about two hours. Strain the mixture into a pitcher and mix in the lemon juice.

48. Catnip Tea

Ingredients:

- 4 cups water
- 2 tablespoons dried catnip leaves

Directions:

1. Bring water to a boil in a medium saucepan over high heat.
2. Remove from the heat and add the catnip leaves. Steep for 10 minutes and strain the catnip leaves. Serve immediately.

49. Dandelion Root Tea

Ingredients:

- Dandelion roots (You can use 4 ½ teaspoons of store-bought dried dandelion roots for this recipe or follow the instructions to find out how to prepare the fresh roots.) 2 cups water
- 1 tablespoon whipping cream or butter
- 1 cinnamon stick (alternatively, use a teaspoon of minced fresh ginger or vanilla extract)
- Sugar or any preferred sweetener

Direction:

1. Wash the root thoroughly under running water to get rid of all the dirt. Then, chop them into smaller pieces to allow them to dry faster. Place them on a clean towel in a dry area until brittle. This process can take three days to a couple of weeks, depending on the thickness of the roots. Alternatively, you can place them in a dehydrator, if available, for 12 hours.

2. Place the dried roots in a pot over medium heat and roast them until golden brown. They will start to smell like baked chocolate chip cookies.

3. Add the water and all your favourite spices and bring it to a boil. Lower the heat and simmer for 45 minutes.

4. Strain the mixture to get rid of the dandelion roots, add butter, cream, sweetener, vanilla extract, or any preferred flavourings and serve.

50. Yarrow Tea

Ingredients:

- 1 tsp. dried yarrow
- Slice of lemon
- 1 c. of boiling water

Direction:

1. Pour boiling water into a mug and add dried yarrow to it.

2. Leave it for about ten minutes to steep.

3. Strain the leaves.

4. Add honey or lemon slices and enjoy.

51. Burdock Tonic Tea

Ingredients:

- Dried peppermint leaves, to taste
- 2 Dried red clover flowers
- 1 tsp Dried dandelion root
- 1 tsp Dried burdock root

Direction:

1. Start by mixing all of the ingredients together and then place them into a large mug.

2. Pour in some boiling water, cover the cup, and let it steep for 30 minutes. Strain and enjoy.

52. Healthy Heart Tea

Ingredients:

- 5 c Cold water,
- 2 pinches Fennel seeds,
- 2 slices Ginger root,
- 1/8 c Hawthorn berries,
- 1 tsp Motherwort,

Direction:

1. Pour the water into a pot and add in all of the herbs. Let this come to a boil, turn the heat down, and simmer for 20 minutes.
2. Let it cool enough to drink, and add in lemon or honey if you want. Enjoy.

53. Herb Robert Tea

Ingredients:

- 2 L of ginger ale
- ¼ c. honey
- ¼ c. orange juice
- ¼ c. lemon juice
- ¼ c. finely chopped fresh mint
- ¼ c. finely chopped lemon balm

Direction:

1. Add the five ingredients into a small bowl.
2. Allow steeping for 1 hour.
3. Strain it and remove the herbs from the mixture.
4. Pour the tea into a pitcher.
5. Add the ginger ale and stir before you serve.

54. Horsetail Tea

Ingredients:

- Honey or sweetener of your choice
- 2 c. hot water
- 3 tsp. dried horsetail

Preparation:

1. Pour water into a pot and bring to boil on a stove. Add the dried horsetail to a teapot.

2. Pour the hot water on the horsetail.

3. Leave the tea to steep for about 10 minutes.

4. Strain the tea and add honey or any sweetener you prefer. Enjoy the tea.

55. Sautéed Chicken of the Woods Mushrooms

Ingredients:

- 1 pound chicken of the wood's mushrooms, sliced
- 2 tablespoons olive oil
- 3 cloves sliced garlic
- 2 chopped shallots
- Salt and pepper
- ½ cup white wine
- 1 lemon's juice
- Chopped parsley

Direction:

1. Heat the olive oil on medium heat in a large skillet and add the mushrooms evenly spaced in the skillet.

2. Cook the mushrooms for about two minutes on each side until golden.

3. Add the shallot and garlic slices, sprinkle some salt and pepper, and mix. Cook for about five minutes until the shallots soften and pour in the white wine.

4. Let the mushrooms absorb the wine for five more minutes.

5. Squeeze some lemon juice on top, sprinkle some chopped parsley, and serve.

56. Mayflower Chicken

Ingredients:

- 1 onion
- 2 chicken breasts
- 200 mills of boiling water
- 5 closed cap mushrooms
- 50 g peas
- 56 g mayflower Chinese curry powder
- 80 g basmati rice
- Low-fat calorie cooking spray

Direction:

1. Chop the chicken breast into small pieces. Also, chop the onion and mushroom into small pieces
2. Spray a saucepan with cooking spray.
3. Add the chicken and allow it to become brown.
4. Add the vegetables to the saucepan and add 200ml hot water to the mayflower curry. Mix well.
5. Add curry sauce to the pan containing the cooked vegetables and chicken. Allow cooking for about 5 minutes. Drain, and then rinse. Serve and enjoy.

57. Chicken Cutlets with Green and Currants Pan Sauce

Ingredients:

- 2 tbsp. extra-virgin olive oil
- Kosher salt and fresh ground pepper
- 8 ⅓-inch chicken cutlets
- 1 small, minced shallot

- 1 ½ c. chicken stock
- ¾ c. pitted green picholine olive
- 1 tsp. Dijon mustard
- 2 ½ tbsp. dried currants
- 2 tbsp. drained capers
- 1 tbsp. cold butter

Direction:

1. Heat the oil in a large skillet and simmer. Add pepper and salt to the chicken cutlets and cook over high heat. Transfer to a plate and place aside.
2. Transfer the shallot to the skillet and cook over medium heat until it is fragrant. Add the stock and continue cooking for another 30 seconds. \Add the mustard and simmer for about 3 minutes.
3. Add capers, olives, and currants and simmer for 1 minute. Transfer the chicken to the skillet and simmer for one more minute.
4. Return the chicken to the plate and put off the heat. Add the butter to the sauce and spread the sauce over the chicken cutlets. Serve and enjoy.

58. Colombian Chicken Stew

Ingredients:

- 1 whole chicken, cut into pieces
- 3 garlic cloves, pressed
- ½ onion, chopped
- 2 teaspoon salt
- 4 lbs. potatoes, peeled and quartered
- 1 ½ cups frozen corn
- 1 bunch scallions
- ½ cup Galinsoga leaves, chopped

Direction:

1. Add chicken to a suitable cooking pot with enough water to cover it.
2. Cook the chicken until soft, then drain and remove the bones.
3. Add potatoes and stock to a cooking pot. Cook on a simmer until potatoes are soft. Cut the chicken into small cubes and the potatoes into slices.
4. Add chicken, potatoes, and remaining ingredients to the stock. Cook for 5 minutes on a simmer. Serve warm.

59. Creamy Lambs Quarter Gratin

Ingredients:

- 1 ½ pounds' lambs-quarters
- 1 bunch of chopped scallions
- Salt
- 1 tbsp. olive oil
- 1 c. milk
- Freshly ground black pepper
- 3 tbsp. unsalted butter
- 3 tbsp. All-purpose flour
- ¼ tsp. nutmeg

Direction:

1. Heat the oven to 350°F and place the rack in the middle. Boil slated water in a large saucepan. Also, wash the lamb's quarters in a bowl using cold water and drain.
2. Cook the lambs' quarter on medium heat until the stems are tender and the leaves are wilted.
3. Drain the greens and rinse well using running cold water. Press out the excess liquid. Once done, chop the greens and pour them into a bowl.

4. Pour the scallion into olive oil and cook, adding a quarter teaspoon of salt.

5. Melt the butter for 2 minutes. Mix the sauce into the green mixture and spread it out in a baking dish.

60. Pork Chops with Barberry (Barberry)

Ingredients:

- 3 c. water
- 6 bone-in centre-cut pork loin chops
- 1 whole star anise pod
- 3 thyme sprigs
- 4 allspice berries
- 4 whole cloves
- 4 Rosemarie
- 1 ½ tbsp. honey
- 1 ½ tbsp. light brown
- 3 ½ tbsp. coarse sea salt

Direction:

1. Add all the ingredients to a medium saucepan, leaving the pork chops.

2. Place on the stove to boil and stir to ensure the salt dissolves. Allow boiling for about 2 minutes. Transfer to a medium bowl and pour ice water into another bowl.

3. Place the brine bowl in an ice bath until it gets cool. Make sure you also stir often. Pour the brine into a bag and seal. Place the pork in a refrigerator for 2 hours.

4. Add the pomegranate juice, honey, and barberries into a medium saucepan.

5. Add the bay leaves, cloves, and thyme sprigs to the cheesecloth and tie them into a bundle. Cover and simmer until it boils for 15 minutes. Allow cooling and serve.

61. Lamb's Quarters Potato Tots

Ingredients:

- 4 fairly-sized baking potatoes (finely peeled)
- ½ cup of cheddar cheese (finely grated)
- ½ cup of mozzarella cheese (finely grated)
- ¼ cup of chopped lamb's quarters
- 1 tsp paprika
- 1 tsp garlic powder
- 2 eggs, beaten
- 1 cup of panko crumbs
- Flour
- Peanut oil

Directions:

1. Boil the potatoes in water and let them cook until tender. Drain and allow to cool for some minutes. Grate the potatoes in a large bowl and pour in the cheese, paprika, garlic powder, lamb's quarters, and salt and pepper to taste.
2. Spread a baking sheet for the potatoes. Roll them into small cylinders before placing them on the baking sheet.
3. Then, start dusting each potato in flour, egg, and panko crumbs one by one. Note that the flour, eggs, and crumbs should be in separate bowls.
4. Place each potato tot on the baking sheets until you finish all. Then, put the sheet inside your refrigerator for 20 to 30 minutes to allow the mixtures to settle in well.
5. After this, cook the tots in your deep fryer until each one is golden brown on all sides. This shouldn't take more than 5 minutes.

6. Drain the soil and serve with vinegar aioli. The lamb's quarters can be replaced with any other edible wild greens such as dandelion, curly dock, Plantago, etc.

62. Lamb's Quarters and Kale

Ingredients:

- 1 box (9 oz.) manicotti shells, cooked
- 2 to 3 cups spaghetti sauce

Filling

- 1 cup Lamb's Quarters, chopped
- 1 cup kale, chopped
- 1 lb. ricotta cheese
- 2 large eggs
- 1 1/2 cups mozzarella cheese, shredded
- 1/2 cup Parmesan cheese, grated
- Salt and black pepper to taste
- Fresh parsley to garnish

Direction:

1. Mix cheese, black pepper, salt, eggs, ricotta, 1 cup mozzarella, parmesan, kale, and Lamb's Quarters in a bowl. Stuff the manicotti shell with cheese mixture.
2. Spread half of the sauce on a baking sheet and place the stuffed pasta in the sauce. Top this pasta with the remaining sauce and cheese on top.

3. Bake the pasta for 30 minutes at 350 degrees F in the oven. Garnish with parsley. Serve warm.

63. Salt and Vinegar Lamb's Quarters

Ingredients:

- 4 cups of freshly picked lamb's quarter's leaves, finely chopped
- 2 tbsps. raw vinegar
- 2 tbsps. olive oil
- ¼ tsp sea salt
- 2 tbsps. of basil, thyme, mint, rosemary, or any other finely chopped fresh herb from the garden (optional)

Direction:

1. The preparation is straightforward. Wash the greens, chop them into fine pieces, and place them all into a large or fairly-sized bowl. Mix in the remaining ingredients and make sure they blend well together. That is all.
2. You can eat the salad fresh or bake it in an oven for 15 to 20 minutes. Be sure to spread the salad on a baking sheet evenly.
3. Go back to the list of edible wild plants suitable for salad and find those you can use to make this healthy salad. You can switch up the edible plants for one another or use a mix of two plants. It depends on what you're looking to achieve.

64. Lamb's Quarter Spread

Ingredients:

- 3 cups Lamb's Quarter leaves, chopped
- 3 garlic cloves, minced
- 1 onion, chopped
- 2 ripe avocados, peeled and pitted
- 1/2 cup toasted nuts or seeds
- 1/4 cup olive oil
- 8 to 16 manzanilla olives
- 3/4 cup chickpeas
- Seasonings to taste

Direction:

1. Blend Lamb's Quarter with onion and garlic in a food processor.
2. Add the rest of the ingredients and blend again until smooth.
3. Serve.

65. Immune Boosting Coffee

Ingredients:

- Pinch of salt
- 4 c Water
- 5 c Coffee
- 1 tbsp Powdered turkey tails
- 1 tbsp Powdered tinder conk
- 1 tbsp Powdered chaga

Direction:

1. Start by adding the water to your drip coffee maker. Place the turkey tail, tinder conk, and chaga into the filter and then add the coffee on top of them.

2. Add in a pinch of salt to help with the bitterness.

3. Brew as you normally work, and sweeten if desired.

66. Dandelion Root Coffee

Ingredients:

- 2 tablespoons roasted Dandelion root
- 1 stick cinnamon
- 1 teaspoon fennel seed
- 2 cups water

Direction:

1. Add water, Dandelion, cinnamon, and fennel seed in a saucepan.

2. Cook this Dandelion mixture for 15 minutes on a simmer.

3. Drain and serve warm.

67. Stinging Nettle Smoothie

Ingredients

- 1 banana
- ½ cucumber
- ½ avocado
- ¼ pineapple
- handful of nettles
- coconut milk, to your desired
- ice

Direction:

1. Add the coconut milk and then the nettles and any other greens you may be using

2. Add the pineapple and the fruits

3. Add the avocado

4. Add ice and then blend

68. Bittercress

Ingredients:

- 2 tsp. of olive oil
- 1 bunch of bittercress
- ½ tsp. red chili flakes
- Kosher salt and pepper
- 3 cloves of garlic
- 1 small onion, minced

Direction:

1. Heat the oil in a saucepan on low heat. Add the red crushed chili flakes, garlic, and onion.

2. Continue cooking until you perceive the aroma.

3. Add the bittercress and increase the heat.

4. Continue stirring until the bittercress wilts and add salt.

5. Serve with vegetables or meat.

69. Pigweed Smoothie (Pigweed)

Ingredients:

- 1 c. coconut water
- Honey or 3 dates as a sweetener

- 1 tbsp. chia seeds
- ½ pear
- ½ apple
- A handful of spinach and pigweed mix

Preparation:

1. Pour the greens into the blender and add coconut water. Then blend until the leaves liquefy.
2. Add the remaining ingredients and blend again until smooth.
3. Serve and enjoy.

70. Aronia Berries Smoothie

Ingredients:

- ½ c. juiced Aronia berries
- Half a banana
- 2 tsp. lemon juice

Direction:

1. Add sugar and water to the berries and boil on a stove.
2. Add pectin and lemon juice. Allow cooling and serve.

71. Cleaver Juice (Cleaver)

Ingredients:

- 1 tbsp. xylitol
- 1 lemon
- 2 large handfuls of cleavers

Direction:

1. Pour the xylitol, lemon, and cleavers into a container.
2. Add water to it and place it in a refrigerator for about 1 week.
3. Strain the extra liquid and transfer it into an air-tight container.
4. Add sparkling water to it and mix. You can also add vodka as a form of refreshment.

72. Crowberry Juice

Ingredients:

- 1 L of raw crowberry juice
- 500g of sugar

Direction:

1. Pour the raw juice into a pot and add sugar.
2. Allow boiling until the sugar dissolves.
3. Leave it to cool and transfer into sterilized bottles.
4. You can store it for up to 12 months. The shelf life increases as the amount of sugar used increases.

73. Forsythia Juice

Ingredients:

- 3 cups filtered water
- 3 cups organic cane sugar
- 3 cups Forsythia flowers

Direction:

1. Add water, cane sugar, and flowers to a cooking pot.
2. Cook to a boil, then remove from the heat.
3. Allow the juice to cool and serve.

74. Honeysuckle Vodka Lemonade

Ingredients:

- 2 cups Honeysuckle blossoms
- 750 ml bottle of vodka
- 1 tablespoon sugar
- 2 cups filtered water
- juice of 2 lemons

Direction:

1. Soak blossoms in vodka for 10 minutes.
2. Mix lemon juice, water, and 1 tbsp sugar in a jug.
3. Strain vodka and add to the lemonade.
4. Serve.

75. Wild-Garlic Salmon

Ingredients

- salmon
- sliced bread with the crusts removed

- 1 garlic clove
- ¼ cup wild garlic leaves
- 1 cup melted butter
- salsa
- ¼ cup wild garlic leaves
- 8 anchovies
- 70ml olive oil
- 1 lemon
- 1 shallot
- 1 tsp capers

Direction:

1. For the crust, put the bread and garlic in a food processor and blend until it becomes fine breadcrumbs. Add the wild garlic and blend for a minute.
2. Add in the butter and blend until it resembles a green dough. Tip it out on a sheet of parchment paper, lay another sheet on top, and roll the dough out. Refrigerate for an hour.
3. Heat the oven to 350°F. Sprinkle salt on the salmon and place it on a tray lined with parchment paper.
4. Take the crust out of the refrigerator and cut it to a similar size as the piece of salmon. Take the parchment paper off and place the crust on top of the salmon.
5. Roast for 20 minutes or until the salmon is cooked all the way through. Place all salsa ingredients in a food processor and blend.
6. Once the salmon is cooked, take it out of the oven and serve with the salsa and lemon wedges.

76. Buffalo Milkweed Pods

Ingredients:

- Favourite hot wing sauce
- Water, .5 c
- Almond milk, .5 c
- Egg
- 1 tsp each Turmeric, cayenne, oregano, and paprika
- 1 tbsp Garlic powder
- 25 c Flour
- 1.5 c Panko
- Milkweed pods

Direction:

1. Start by getting your oven to 350.
2. Combine all of your dry ingredients together.
3. Beat together the water, almond milk, and egg together and then mix it into the dry ingredients. Combine well.
4. Dip the milkweed pods into the batter and then lay them out on a baking sheet that has been lined with parchment. Let them bake for 15 to 20 minutes.
5. Once they are crisp, move them to a bowl. Pour in your favourite wing sauce and make sure that they are well coated. Spread them back out on the baking sheet and cook them for another ten minutes. Enjoy.

77. Dandy Pasta

Ingredients:

- 2 tbsp Favourite spice mixture,
- 3 tbsp Coconut oil
- 25 c Butter
- 2 cloves Garlic

- Red onion
- 2 to 3 c Dandelions with roots
- 2 c Bowtie pasta

Direction:

1. Start by cutting the roots off of the leaves right at the top so that the leaves will stay together. Finely chop up the roots along with the garlic and onion.
2. As this cook, follow the directions on the packaging for your pasta and cook the pasta until done.
3. Melt your butter in a pan along with the coconut oil. Add in the spices and mix well. Add the dandelion root, onion, and garlic, and let this cook for five to ten minutes.
4. After it is done cooking, add in the cooked pasta and stir everything together. Let this simmer together for one to two minutes. Mix in the dandelion leaves. Let it simmer for a minute and enjoy.

78. Ramp Pasta with Morels

Ingredients:

Pasta

- 10 oz. all-purpose flour
- 4 1/2 oz. blanched Ramp leaves

Morel ragu

- 1 lb. fresh Morels
- 1/2 lbs. Ramps, leaves and bulbs separated
- 3 tablespoons butter
- Salt, to taste
- 1/4 teaspoon caraway seed

- 1 cup mushroom broth
- Black pepper to taste

Direction:

1. Boil Ramp leaves in a pot filled with water for 2 minutes, then drain. Puree these leaves with ½ cup water in a blender.
2. Add flour, then mix well to make a smooth dough. Knead this dough for 5 minutes on a floured surface.
3. Divide the dough into 6 equal pieces and spread each portion into a 1/8-inch-thick sheet. Cut each sheet into spaghetti one after another. Sauté Morels with Ramps and butter in a skillet for 5 minutes.
4. Stir in salt, caraway seed, black pepper, and broth, then cook to a boil. Stir in spaghetti, then cook for 5 minutes.
5. Serve warm.

79. Purslane Egg Cups

Ingredients:

- Favourite spices
- 25 c Cheddar cheese
- 12 Eggs
- 25 c Milk
- 2 Finely chopped onions
- Small pepper, chopped
- 2 c Chopped purslane

Direction:

1. Start by making sure your oven is at 350. Take a muffin pan and grease it well.

2. In a pan with some butter, add the pepper and onion and sauté for about five minutes.

3. Using a food processor or blender, add the spices of your choosing, milk, eggs, and cheese. One the pepper and onions are cooked, add those in as well. Blend everything together.

4. Pour into a bowl and stir in the purslane and any other wild greens you would like to use.

5. Divide the egg mixture between the cups in the muffin pan and bake for 20 to 25 minutes, or until the eggs are completely cooked.

80. Dandelion Banana Bread

Ingredients:

- 5 tsp baking soda
- 1 tsp baking powder
- 33 c Dandelion flower petals
- 1.25 c Flour,
- 33 c Brown sugar
- Egg
- 5 c Olive oil
- Ripe banana

Direction:

1. Start by mashing up the banana and mixing in the sugar, egg, and oil. Stir in the baking soda, baking powder, dandelion flowers, and flour.

2. Mix until everything comes together. If you want, you can also add chocolate chips or walnuts.

3. Scoop into a greased loaf pan.

4. Bake for 20 to 25 minutes at 350.

5. Once cooked through, slice and enjoy.

81. White Clover Pudding (Clover)

Ingredients:

- 2 c. white clover blossoms
- 1 c. water
- 1 tbsp. organic unflavoured gelatine
- ½ c. fresh orange juice
- 1 c. stiff heavy cream
- 4 tbsp. white clover honey
- Pinch of salt

Direction:

1. Add the gelatine to a quarter cup of water to dissolve. Pour the white clover blossoms into a small saucepan and place them on a low heat to boil. Add salt, honey, orange juice, and water to it.

2. Turn off the heat and continue stirring the gelatine to dissolve completely. Then leave it for about 10 minutes. Cover and place in the fridge to allow the gelatine to firm.

3. Add heavy cream and mix until the mixture becomes stiff. Place it into a serving bowl and return to the fridge to allow it to set.

82. Raspberry Pie

Ingredients:

- 200 g chopped unsalted butter
- 400 g dark chocolate
- 30 g top-quality cocoa
- ½ c. sunflower oil

- 1 c. brown sugar
- ½ c. caster sugar
- 1 tsp. vanilla extract
- 3 eggs
- 1 ½ c. plain sifted flour
- 1 c. buttermilk
- ½ tsp. baking powder
- 250 g raspberries

Direction:

1. Preheat the oven to 160°C. Coat the side of the lamington pan with grease and cover with baking paper.
2. Add oil, chocolate, cocoa, and butter to a bowl and set on a pan to simmer.
3. Add eggs, vanilla, and sugar to another bowl and whisk: mix salt flakes, baking powder, buttermilk, and flour in the melted chocolate. Then fold in half of the raspberries.
4. Spread batter in a pan and place the raspberries on it.
5. Allow baking for 1 hour and 30 minutes.
6. Cool in the pan and place in the fridge for 30 minutes. Slice to serve.

83. Watercress Pot Pies

Ingredients:

- 2 cups watercress, chopped
- 1 tablespoon garlic, minced
- 1 celery stalk, finely chopped
- 2 teaspoons fresh thyme, finely chopped
- 2 tablespoons butter
- 1 onion, finely chopped

- 3 carrots, finely chopped
- 6 cups chicken broth
- 1 tablespoon fresh parsley, finely chopped
- Salt and pepper to taste
- 4 pie crusts

Directions:

1. Combine watercress, garlic, celery, and thyme in a large pot. Add butter and cook over medium heat until the butter is melted.
2. Stir in onion and carrots. Cook for 4-6 minutes, until the onions are soft.
3. Pour in broth and bring to a boil over high heat. Reduce heat and simmer for 15 minutes until the carrots are soft.
4. Season with parsley, salt, and pepper to taste.
5. Preheat the oven to 375°F.
6. Pour broth mixture into 4 oven-safe bowls and let cool for 15 minutes. Roll out pie crusts and cut out the tops of the bowls, leaving a ½-inch overhang.
7. Lightly brush the edges of each bowl with water and place the pie crust on top. Use a fork to press the edges together and cut 2-3 slits in the top of each pot pie.
8. Bake for 20 minutes or until the crust is browned and cooked through. Serve immediately.

84. Plum and Mascarpone Pie

Ingredients:

- 1 pie crust
- 5 pounds of firm-ripe plums
- 1 ½ c. sugar
- 2 tbsp. fresh lemon juice

- 1 vanilla bean
- 8 oz. mascarpone
- ⅓ c. crème Fraiche
- 2 tbsp. honey
- Whipped cream

Direction:

1. Preheat the oven to 350°F. Line the pie dish with crust.
2. Place the plums in a large bowl and add one and a half cups of lemon and sugar.
3. Divide the plum mixture into 2 baking dishes and roast for about 60 minutes.
4. Transfer the plum to a baking sheet and transfer the juices to a baking dish. Boil for about 5 minutes.
5. Add the remaining sugar, honey, crème Fraiche and mascarpone to a bowl. Add seeds from vanilla beans and beat at high speed. Spread the mascarpone cream evenly. Spread some glaze over the plums. C
6. Put the pie into slices and spread whipped cream on it. Serve and enjoy.

85. Strawberry-Knotweed Pie

Ingredients:

- 1 9" pie crust
- Filling 4 cups strawberries
- 2 cups trimmed Japanese Knotweed stalks
- 3/4 cups white sugar

- 1/4 cup corn-starch
- 1/4 teaspoon salt

Direction:

1. Cook strawberries with Knotweed stalks, white sugar, salt and corn-starch in a saucepan.
2. Stir well and cook until the strawberries are soft. Mash them lightly then remove from the heat. Spread the pie crust in a pie plate.
3. Bake for about 20-25 minutes in the oven at 350 degrees F. Add the filling to the centre of the baked crust. Serve.

86. Passion Fruit and Lemon Condensed Milk Slice (Passion Fruit)

Ingredients:

- 14 digestive biscuits
- 2 395g cans of sweetened condensed milk
- 185 ml of strained fresh lemon juice
- 125 ml of fresh passion fruit pulp

Direction:

1. Preheat the oven to 160°C. Line a pan with baking paper.
2. Arrange the biscuits on the base of the pan, keeping 2 biscuits aside.
3. Add the lemon juice, condensed milk, and passion fruit juice pump together in a bowl and whisk. Pour the mixture over the biscuits and bake for 15 minutes.
4. Allow to cool at room temperature and put in the fridge overnight.

87. Cranberry Sauce

Ingredients:

- 1 c. sugar
- 4 c. fresh or frozen cranberries
- 1 c. water

optional

- Pecans, orange zest, currants, raisins, nutmeg, cinnamon, etc.

Direction:

1. Rinse the cranberries using clean water and remove any damaged ones among them. Add sugar to the water and boil in a medium saucepan until the sugar dissolves.
2. Add the cranberries to the boiling water and cook until the cranberries burst.
3. Add any of the optional ingredients to dress it.
4. Allow cooling and serve.

88. Fireweed Sauce

Ingredients:

- 40 Pink Clover flowers
- 30 White Clover flowers
- 50 Fireweed flowers
- 1/2 teaspoon alum
- 5 lbs organic cane sugar
- 3 cups boiling water

Direction:

1. Add flowers, alum, cane sugar and water to a cooking pot.

2. Cook to a boil, then allow the mixture to cool.

3. Strain and serve.

89. Highbush Cranberry Sauce

Ingredients:

- 3 cups Highbush Cranberries
- 1 cup organic cane sugar
- 2 teaspoons orange zest
- juice of 1 orange

Direction:

1. Add cranberries, sugar, orange zest and juice to a saucepan.

2. Cook the berries to a boil, then simmer for 20 minutes until soft.

3. Mash the berries and serve.

90. Yellow Dock Seed Crackers

Ingredients:

- 1 cup crushed Yellow Dock seed
- 1 cup flour
- 1 teaspoon sea salt

Direction:

1. Mix Yellow Dock seeds with salt and flour in a mixing bowl.

2. Stir in water and mix well to make a dough.

3. Spread the dough into a 1/8-inch-thick sheet, then cut into triangles.

4. Place these pieces on a baking sheet, then bake for 12 minutes at 375 degrees Fahrenheit.

5. Flip once cooked halfway through. Serve.

91. Dandelion & Honey Ice Cream

Ingredients:

- 1 1/2 cups heavy cream
- 1 1/2 cups half and half
- 1/2 cup honey
- 1 cup Dandelion petals
- 1 pinch sea salt
- 6 egg yolks

Direction:

1. Mix heavy cream with half and half, honey, Dandelion, and salt in a saucepan.

2. Cook this mixture to a simmer, then remove from the heat.

3. Leave this mixture for 30 minutes, then drain.

4. Blend this mixture with egg yolks in a blender, then transfer to an ice-cream machine.

5. Churn as per the machine's instruction, then refrigerate for 4 hours. Serve.

92. Strawberry White Clover Cookies

Ingredients:

- 1 cup butter, softened
- ¾ cup brown sugar, packed
- 2 eggs
- 2 tablespoons milk
- 3 cups all-purpose flour
- 1 teaspoon baking soda
- ½ cup fresh White Clover blossoms, chopped
- 1 cup strawberries, dice

Direction:

1. Preheat your oven at 350 degrees F. Layer a cookie sheet with parchment paper.
2. Mix flour, eggs, milk, brown sugar, butter, baking soda, and clover in a bowl to make a smooth dough.
3. Fold in strawberries and knead the dough. Drop the dough spoon by spoon over the cookie sheet.
4. Next bake the White Clover cookies for 15 minutes until golden brown.
5. Allow the cookies to cool, then serve.

93. Almond Fairy Cakes with Candied Borage Flowers

Ingredients:

Candied Flowers:

- 36 fresh Borage flowers, rinsed and dried
- 1 pasteurized egg white

- Granulated sugar, to taste

Fairy Cakes

- 1 cup cake flour
- 1/4 cup almond flour
- 1/2 teaspoon baking powder
- 1/4 teaspoon salt
- 1/2 cup granulated sugar
- 1 stick (1/2 cup) unsalted butter
- 2 large eggs
- 1/4 cup whole milk
- 1 teaspoon vanilla extract
- 3/4 teaspoon almond extract

Fondant

- 2 1/2 cups granulated sugar
- 1/2 cup water
- 1/4 cup corn syrup
- 1/4 teaspoon almond extract

Direction:

1. Beat sugar with egg white in a bowl, then dip the flowers in it to coat.
2. Spread the coated flowers on a baking sheet and set it aside.
3. Mix and blend all the cake ingredients in a mixing bowl.
4. Divide this batter into a muffin tray lined with paper liners.
5. Bake the cupcakes for 20 minutes until golden brown.
6. Meanwhile, beat sugar, water, corn syrup and almond extract in a bowl with a beater to make a smooth fondant.
7. Divide and spread the fondant over the cupcakes. Garnish each cupcake with candied flowers. Serve.

94. Chokecherry Syrup

Ingredients:

- Chokecherry
- Sugar
- Lemon juice
- Orange juice
- Pectin

Direction:

1. Wash the chokecherry thoroughly and add to a saucepan. Cover with water.
2. Boil the chokeberries for about 30 minutes.
3. Strain the juice in it into a separate container and cover it.
4. Add some sugar to it. Next, add lemon juice and orange.
5. Add pectin and mix over medium heat for about 30 minutes.
6. Cool in the refrigerator. Transfer it to a jar and process in boiling water for about 10 minutes.

95. Bee Balm Cookies

Ingredients:

- 4 tsp orange zest,
- 4 to 5 tbsp Chopped bee balm flowers and leaves
- 1 c Flour
- 5 c Powdered sugar
- 5 c Butter

Direction:

1. Start by beating the butter with the bee balm, sugar, and orange zest until well combined. Add in the flour and mix together. You may have to use your hands to really get it mixed together because it will get thick. Make sure you don't overwork the dough once you add the flour. Once smooth, roll into a cylinder and wrap in parchment. Chill for two hours.

2. Once chilled, slice the dough into quarter-inch slices. Place them on a baking sheet about an inch apart.

3. Bake for eight to ten minutes at 350. Enjoy.

96. Fennel and Angelica Cookies

Ingredients:

- 2.5 c Flour
- 1 tbsp Fennel seeds
- 2 tbsp Chopped angelica leaves
- Light beaten egg yolk
- 5 to .75 c Sugar
- 1 c Butter

Direction:

1. Start by adding the butter and sugar to a bowl and mix well. Stir in the angelica and egg yolk. Slowly add in the flour and fennel. Stir everything together so that it is well combined.

2. Once blended, cover, and refrigeration for 30 minutes.

3. Get your oven to 375 and place some parchment paper on some baking sheets.

4. Take the dough out and roll golf ball sizes of dough between your hands. Flatten them out on the parchment to eighth of an inch thick. You can also roll the dough out and use cookie cutters if you would prefer.

5. Bake for 12 to 15 minutes. Let them cool for ten minutes and then place them on a wire rack to cool completely.

97. Wild Potato Pancakes

Ingredietns:

- 1 tsp Pepper,
- 1 tsp Salt,
- 2 tsp Garlic powder,
- 2 tbsp Flour
- 2 tbsp Hemp seeds
- 25 c Chopped mushrooms
- 5 c Chopped wild greens
- 33 c Chopped onions
- 2 Eggs
- 4 c Grated potatoes

Direction:

1. Start by melting some butter in a pan. Add the onions and sauté for a couple of minutes and then mix in the mushrooms. Cook for another two minutes and set it off of the heat.

2. In a bowl, add the spices, flour, seeds, eggs, sautéed vegetables, and grated potatoes. Mix everything together for about three minutes to make sure everything is well combined.

3. In a frying pan, melt a bit of butter to make sure the pancakes don't stick. With your hands, create balls from the batter. As you do this, you will notice that the potatoes contain some liquid. Squeeze out some of this liquid.

4. Lay the ball onto the frying pan and flatten it with a spatula to about a half-inch thick. Cook until both sides are golden brown. Add extra butter if you need to so that they don't stick.

5. Continue until all of the batter is used and enjoy.

98. Cloudberry Cake

Ingredients:

- Unsalted butter
- ¾ c. cake flour
- 1 c. granulated sugar
- 6 large eggs
- 1 tsp. baking powder
- Fresh edible flowers
- 1 pt. fresh blackberries
- 1 pt. resin raspberries
- 3 c. cloudberry jam
- 2 tsp. pure vanilla extract
- 4 tbsp. confectionary sugar
- 3 c. heavy cream

Direction:

1. Preheat the oven to 350°F.
1. Cover the sides of a pan using parchment paper.
2. Brush the pan with butter and sprinkle flowers on it.
3. Add the baking powder and cake flour to a bowl.
4. Add the egg white to a bowl and whisk. Then add salt and granulated sugar.
5. Divide the batter and bake for 20 minutes. Bring it out and let it cool for another 20 minutes.
6. Split the cake horizontally and serve.

99. Blackcaps Pudding

Ingredients:

- 6 dessert apples
- 2 tbsp. sugar
- 1 tbsp. orange flower water
- Drizzle of Grand Marnier

Direction:

1. Wash the apples and slice them to prevent them from popping. Sprinkle it with sugar.
2. Place the apples in a baking tray and cover them with orange flower water.
3. Place in the oven and bake at 200°C for 30 minutes.
4. After removing it from the oven, sprinkle with sugar and add the Grand Marnier.
5. Put back in the oven. Leave in the oven for another 30 minutes, after which the apples must look blackened.

100.   Violet Jelly

Ingredients:

- 3 cups Violet blooms
- juice of 1 lemon
- 2 ½ cups boiling water
- 1 package of pectin
- 3 1/2 cups sugar

Direction:

1. Soak Violet blossoms in 2 ½ cups boiling water in a bowl for 10 minutes.

2. Strain and add lemon juice, sugar, and pectin to the water.

3. Pour the water into a shallow bowl.

4. Allow the jelly to set.

5. Slice and serve.

101.   Summertime Jelly

Ingredients:

- 2 cups fresh Queen Anne's Lace flowers

- 4 cups water

- 1/4 cup lemon juice

- 1 package powdered pectin

- 3 1/2 cups plus

- 2 tablespoons organic cane sugar

Direction:

1. Add water, lemon juice, pectin, cane sugar and flowers to a saucepan.

2. Cook this mixture to a boil, remove from the heat, then strain into a bowl.

3. Cover and leave this mixture for 1½ hours.

4. Serve.

102.   Stinging Nettle Spanakopita

Ingredients:

- 8 cups fresh Stinging Nettle leaves

- 2 tablespoons melted butter
- 3/4 cups scallions, chopped
- 1 1/2 cup crumbled feta cheese
- 1/2 cup Parmesan cheese, grated
- 2 eggs, beaten
- 1/3 cup parsley, chopped
- ¼ teaspoon grated nutmeg
- 18 organic phyllo sheets
- ½ cup melted butter

Direction:

1. Boil Nettle leaves in a pot filled with water for 3-5 minutes, then drain. Sauté scallions with 2 tablespoons butter in a wok for 2 minutes.

2. Stir in Nettle and cook for 5 minutes. Remove from this wok from the heat.

3. Stir in nutmeg, parsley, egg, feta, and parmesan. Grease a 9x13 inch baking pan with melted butter.

4. Unroll phyllo and brush each sheet with butter. Stack 4 sheets over another.

5. Place them in the prepared pan and add the nettle mixture on top. Stack the remaining phyllo sheet over the filling.

6. Brush the top with butter and cut into 12 pieces. Bake the pieces for 45 minutes in the oven until golden brown. Serve.

REFERENCES

A fall field guide: Foraging for nuts. (n.d.). Mother Earth News. Retrieved from https://www.motherearthnews.com/sustainable-living/nature-and-environment/foraging-for-nuts-zmaz88sozgoe/

Adamant, A., 2019. 50+ edible wild berries & fruits ~ A foragers guide. Practical Self Reliance. Adapted from; https://practicalselfreliance.com/edible-wild-berries-fruits/

Avoid poisonous plants when working outdoors, 2016. Safety+Health Magazine. Adapted from: https://www.safetyandhealthmagazine.com/articles/14289-avoid-poisonous-plants-when-working-outdoors

Cattail soup recipe. (n.d.). Ediblewildfood.Com. Retrieved from https://www.ediblewildfood.com/cattail-soup.aspx Chicken of the Woods: Your guide to Laetiporus sulphureus. (n.d.). Whyfarmit.Com. Retrieved from https://whyfarmit.com/chicken-of-the-woods/

Daisy Coyle, A. P. D. (2018, April 4). Top 7 health benefits of asparagus. Healthline. https://www.healthline.com/nutrition/asparagus-benefits

Dessinger, H., 2021. Roasted dandelion root tea recipe and benefits. Retrieved from: Mommypotamus. https://mommypotamus.com/dandelion-tea/

Engels, J., 2021. Fruits and nuts to find in fall. One Green Planet: https://www.onegreenplanet.org/lifestyle/fruits-nuts-find-fall/ Foraging: Ultimate guide to wild food.

Filippone, P. T. (n.d.). Edible mushroom varieties. Retrieved from The Spruce Eats website: https://www.thespruceeats.com/edible-mushroom-varieties-1807698

Garcia, E., 2021. Winter foraging: 20+ edible greens, nuts, seeds, and fruits to forage for in cold weather. Insteading. https://insteading.com/blog/winter-foraging/

Guide to poisonous plants. (n.d.). WebMD. Retrieved from https://www.webmd.com/skin-problems-and-treatments/ss/slideshow-poison-plants-guide

Hardlikearmour, 2011. Pan-fried dandelion flowers. Food52. https://food52.com/recipes/11680-pan-fried-dandelion-flowers H

Lambert, R., 2018. Foraging as a way to feel connected. Wild Walks Southwest. https://www.wildwalks-southwest.co.uk/foraging-as-a-way-to-feel-connected/

MacWelch, T., 2019. 13 toxic wild plants that look like food. Outdoor Life. https://www.outdoorlife.com/13-toxic-wild-plants-not-food/

Norris, M., 2019. 5 rules for foraging wild edibles + 25 wild edible plants. Melissa K. Norris. https://melissaknorris.com/podcast/5rulesforagingwildedibles/

Raman, R., MS, & RD., 2020). 10 tasty wild berries to try (and 8 poisonous ones to avoid). Healthline. https://www.healthline.com/nutrition/wild-berries

Rezackova, L., 2020. 7 amazing benefits of foraging for wild foods. Creativeedgetravel. https://www.creativeedgetravel.com/post/7-amazing-benefits-of-foraging-for-wild-foods

Stull, J. (n.d.). Poisonous plants: How to deal. Outdoor Project. Retrieved from https://www.outdoorproject.com/articles/poisonous-plants-how-deal

The difference between flowers & weeds. 2010. Retrieved from Sciencing website: https://sciencing.com/the-difference-between-flowers-weeds-13428135.html

Turner, P., 2017. 8 edible plants (and their killer cousins!). Adventure Equipped. https://www.adventuremedicalkits.com/blog/2017/10/8-edible-plants-killer-cousins/

Tyrant Farms. https://www.tyrantfarms.com/beginners-guide-to-foraging-rules-to-follow/

Viljoen, M., 2019. These 10 invasive plant species are surprisingly delicious. Saveur. https://www.saveur.com/invasive-edible-weeds/

Printed in Great Britain
by Amazon

34541308R00096